Timeless Writings - 36

Different Authors

Tatay Jobo Elizes
Compiler
Sept. 2017

Published by Tatay Jobo Elizes, Self-Publisher

This book is published and printed under the expressed permission of the various authors compiled for this purpose of making their articles and essays available to the public and promote reading among Filipinos, young and old. They own the copyrights to their writings. Authors can ask to withdraw their writings here anytime and will be edited out in next printing. Printing of this book is using the present day method of Print-On-Demand (POD) system, where prints will never run out of copies. Authors are free to republish or reprint with other publishers and printers anytime.

ISBN Codes

ISBN – 13: 978 – 1976101878 and
ISBN – 10: 1976101875

Disclaimer: Views are expressed by the authors alone. Tatay Jobo Elizes does not knowingly publish false information and may not be held liable for the views of the authors exercising their right to free expression.

Self-Publisher's Details:
Contact: job_elizes@yahoo.com
Websites: http:tinyurl.com/mj76ccq +
www.jobelizes6.wix.com/mysite

Contents

ooooo

1

4th Email: The Disgrace to Lawyers and Economists if Allowed to Continue: Free-Market-Competition Hoax in WESM

Posted by Marcelo Tecson
"martecson"
July 15, 2017

To: "Pres. Rodrigo Duterte c/o PACE"
<pace_op@malacanang.gov.ph>,
Senate President Koko Pimentel
<kokopimenteloffice@yahoo.com>,
Senator Win Gatchalian
<email@wingatchalian.com>,
ERC OIC Commissioner Alfredo Non
<ajnon@erc.gov.ph>,
ERC Commissioner Geronimo Sta. Ana"
<gdstaana@erc.gov.ph>,
ERC Commissioner Josefina Patricia Asirit
<jpmasirit@erc.gov.ph>,
ERC Commissioner Gloria Victoria Yap-
Taruc <gvcyaptaruc@erc.gov.ph>,
DOE Sec Alfonso Cusi
<alfonso.cusi@doe.gov.ph>,
"sensonnyangara@yahoo.com"
"migszubiri2016@yahoo.com.ph"
<migszubiri2016@yahoo.com.ph>,
"ralphgrecto@gmail.com"
<ralphgrecto@gmail.com>,

"senalanpetercayetano1028@gmail.com"
<senalanpetercayetano1028@gmail.com>,
"sen.escudero@gmail.com"
<sen.escudero@gmail.com>,
"gracepoe2013@gmail.com"
<gracepoe2013@gmail.com>,
"os_frankdrilon@yahoo.com"
<os_frankdrilon@yahoo.com>,
"os_sotto@yahoo.com"
<os_sotto@yahoo.com>,
"kiko.pangilinan@gmail.com"
<kiko.pangilinan@gmail.com>,
"sensonnyangara@yahoo.com"
<sensonnyangara@yahoo.com>,
"team.bamaquino@senado.ph"
<team.bamaquino@senado.ph>,
"sen.edpacquiao@gmail.com"
<sen.edpacquiao@gmail.com>,
"binaynancy2013@yahoo.com"
<binaynancy2013@yahoo.com>,
"senatorrichardgordon@gmail.com"
<senatorrichardgordon@gmail.com>,
"loren@lorenlegarda.com.ph"
<loren@lorenlegarda.com.ph>,
"appointments@osl.ph"
<appointments@osl.ph>,
"senate.office.trillanes@gmail.com"
<senate.office.trillanes@gmail.com>,
"sencynthiavillar@gmail.com"
sencynthiavillar@gmail.com
> Cc: "Vice Pres. Rep. Leni Robredo"
 <lenirobredo@gmail.com>,
VP Leni Robredo
<lenirobredo.ovp@gmail.com>,
DOF Sec Carlos Dominguez

<cdominguez@dof.gov.ph>,
DOJ Sec Vitaliano Aguirre II
<osec@doj.gov.ph>,
EcoPlanning Sec Ernesto Pernia
<EMPernia@neda.gov.ph>,
DBM Sec Benjamin Diokno
<bediokno@dbm.gov.ph>,
DPWH Sec Mark Villar
<villar.mark@dpwh.gov.ph>,
DOTC Sec Arthur Tugade
<osec@dotc.gov.ph>,
DA Sec Emmanuel Pinol
<osec.da@gmail.com>,
DTI Sec Ramon Lopez
<RamonLopez@dti.gov.ph>,
DTI Secretary <Secretary@dti.gov.ph>,
PCC Chairman Arsenio Balisacan
<ambalisacan@phcc.gov.ph>,
DOE Helen Arias
<hbarias.eumb@gmail.com>,
Enrico San Juan
culdesac0002@yahoo.com.ph

Subject: 4th Email: THE DISGRACE TO LAWYERS AND ECONOMISTS IF ALLOWED TO CONTINUE: FREE-MARKET-COMPETITION HOAX IN WESM
Reply-To: Marcelo Tecson
martecson@yahoo.com

DEBUNKING THE MYTH OF COMPETITION IN THE EPIRA-DEREGULATED POWER GENERATION OLIGOPOLY

THE SMOKING GUN OF LACK OF COMPETITION IN THE EPIRA-DEREGULATED POWER GENERATION OLIGOPOLY: WESM BIDDING SYSTEM THAT IS SIMPLY RIDICULOUS AND DEVOID OF COMPETITION—IT IS A GAME OF CHANCE!

THERE IS SIMPLY NO PRICE-LOWERING FREE-MARKET COMPETITION IN THE TOUTED WESM BIDDING SCHEME THAT DECLARES AS WINNING BID THE QUOTED HIGHEST PRICE— AND THIS IS DONE EVEN IF THERE ARE SUBMITTED BUT IGNORED MUCH LOWER BIDS—A MOCKERY OF COMPETITIVE BIDDING SYSTEM!

To Begin with, Who are Behind the EPIRA-Mandated Wholesale Electricity Spot Market (WESM)?

Quotes from economist Solita Monsod's "Get Real" column in the Philippine Daily Inquirer on December 13, 2014, page A12, "Who's responsible for power price spike?":

"The Epira (Electric Power Industry Reform Act) of 2001 mandated the Department of Energy (DOE) to establish the Wholesale Electricity Spot Market (WESM) that would 'facilitate a transparent and reliable market for electricity, and, jointly with the electric power industry participants, formulate the detailed rules for the WESM.' This the DOE did, with inputs from the industry participants.

"The Epira also entrusted to the Energy Regulatory Commission (ERC) the approval of the price determination methodology, which it did with the proper consultation.

"An 'autonomous group market operator,' the Philippine Electricity Market Corp. (PEMC) composed of industry participants—involved in generation, transmission, and distribution—was also created, chaired by the DOE. Its role was to 'procure necessary infrastructure and technology, and achieve institutional and participant readiness for the commercial operation of the WESM.' With the DOE as chair, the board members of PEMC, aside from the ERC, are representatives of the generators, transmitters and distributors, plus four independent members (presumably representing consumers).

"I bring this out to show that the government was very visible in making the market rules (WESM)."

(It is obvious that there have been no representatives or inputs from known consumer groups in the formulation and implementation of the WESM rules, a blatant lack of protection to consumers. --M. L. Tecson)

JUST WHAT IS WRONG WITH THE WHOLESALE ELECTRICITY SPOT MARKET (WESM)?

Based on media reports and commentaries, WESM operates a ridiculous game-of-chance procurement bidding system, under which whatever is the last quoted price in the hourly batch of bids— even if it is the HIGHEST bid price, and even if there is a zero-amount bid quotation—becomes the WINNING BID! (Solita Collas-Monsod, "Get Real:

Who's responsible for power price spike?" Philippine Daily Inquirer, December 14, 2013, page A12).

Under the outlandish WESM bidding rules, the winning suppliers and bid prices are separately determined, a ridiculous deviation from the conventional method where the bidder which submitted the lowest bid price becomes the winning supplier. In WESM, the two modes of bidding competition are as follows:

The bidder which submitted the lowest bid rate becomes the winning supplier, from which the needed power supply will be purchased. This explains why some bidders submitted bids at zero price. (The bidding will of course turn to naught or absurdity if all bidders would submit zero bid rates.)

As presented herein later, as Meralco lawyer Victor Lazatin himself in effect indirectly admitted during oral arguments before the Supreme Court in February 2014, on the contested P4.15 per kWh Meralco rate increase reportedly approved by ERC in one hearing session, the winning bid is determined not based on merit but by mere expeditious if illogical mechanics where whichever is the bid price of the last bid in the hourly batch of bids becomes the winning bid rate even if it is the highest bid price, to be applied to the sales-volume offer of the winning lowest bidder, such as the one which submitted the zero bid rate per kWh.

Frankly, is this media-reported bidding scheme not an insane method, an insult to the intelligence of all executive and legislative government officials concerned, as well as victimized economic and finance experts among private power consumers?

In the briefing conducted by ERC on February 9, 2017 at the request of United Filipino Consumers and Commuters (UFCC), held at the ERC offices in Ortigas Center in Pasig City, the lecturing ERC technical staff confirmed that, indeed, the last bid in the hourly batch of bids becomes the winning bid rate for the power to be purchased from the winning bidder with lowest bid price, even if there are much lower bid rates submitted to WESM.

I suppose there is no similar procurement bidding scheme anywhere in the world where the highest bid price—despite available lowest and most advantageous bid offer—becomes the winning bid. This utter lack of free-market competition—and sanity?—in WESM is simply outrageous.

While normal power generation rate shown in Meralco bills is less than P6.00 per kWh, the WESM offer price cap was set at the atrociously high P62.00 per kWh in June 2006. Owing to the prevalence of this ultra high price cap as winning bid even during times of low demand—sign of defective WESM bidding system—the price cap was reduced to P32.00 per kWh in December 2013.

While the Department of Trade and Industry (DTI) runs after profiteering merchants who take advantage of supply shortfall during emergency periods, WESM operators allow WESM bids at the foregoing allowable peak rate whenever there is power supply shortfall brought about by scheduled and unscheduled power plant shutdowns. This improper profiteering scheme is possible because the power generation industry is deregulated under EPIRA and unwisely freed from the Supreme-Court ruled 12% reasonable return on investment. Even then, WESM founders and operators should have exercised simple common sense and proper sense of balance—through setting competitively much lower WESM offer price cap close to P6.00 per kWh. Better still, there should be separate price cap per type of power plant (hydro, geothermal, oil-fired, etc), each with unique generation cost.

The WESM bidding system is evil, a free-market- competition hoax foisted upon blatantly deceived consumers; a mockery of competitive bidding system; and a scheme instituted by the government's Department of Energy and Energy Regulatory Commission that reflects badly on legal, economic, and financial experts in government—especially those who have been in Malacanang, NEDA, DOE, ERC, and Commission on Audit (COA)—who appear blissfully ignorant of, or helpless against, consequently overpriced WESM electricity rate, which victimizes both the government and the paying public in their capacity as overcharged power consumers.

PROOF OF LACK OF TRUE COMPETITION IN WESM

"In power, as in any other sector or industry, competition is what drives the economy to efficiency and improved consumer welfare, a fundamental principle taught in basic economics. Lack of it leads to excessive unearned profits accruing to a few at the expense of the many (that is, we consumers)...." (Cielito F. Habito, "Wanted: true competition in power," Philippine Daily Inquirer, January 21, 2014, page A9).

In the light of such plain and basic economic thought, it is shocking how past and present DOE and ERC officials could play the principal role in the formulation, approval, institution, and perpetuation of the WESM bidding scheme, which is simply ridiculous and devoid of competition.

In procurement, the aim of competitive bidding is to award the purchase to the bidder who submitted the LOWEST bid price, which, with all other things being equal, equates to the most advantageous bid.

In the WESM procurement bidding system, there is clearly no competition for the needed lowest bid price. It declares as WINNING bid the accepted HIGHEST bid—and the winning HIGHEST bid is applied to all power sold, even if there are much LOWER bids!

Even if the winning highest bid price is offered for a small volume by a relatively small power producer, it will be applied to all power sold—a senseless case of the tail wagging the dog and a fertile ground for price manipulation.

How exalted DOE and ERC officials could approve and tolerate such anti-market, anti-business, anti-poor, and anti-reason WESM procurement bidding system is astounding and puzzling. In fact, even Meralco's own lawyer found it improper and indirectly admitted the impropriety before the Supreme Court.

Meralco's Own Lawyer Exposed Before the Supreme Court the Lack of Price-Lowering Competition in WESM:

He in Effect Admitted that in its Bidding System,

Even if there are Submitted Bids at LOWER Rates, these are Deliberately Disregarded and the Accepted HIGHEST Price is Chosen as Winning Bid

Rate—Just What Convoluted Logic Justified this Inanity?

"In the WESM, the sellers of electricity are not paid what they ask for; they are paid what the last accepted bidder asks for. (Their bids are arranged from lowest to highest, and the highest accepted price is what is paid by the consumers. So if the maximum bid of P62/kWh is the clearing price, think of the price spike for the consumers and the windfall profits for some power generators." (Solita Collas-Monsod, "Get Real: Who's responsible for power price spike?" Philippine Daily Inquirer, December 14, 2013, page A12).

Economist Solita Monsod's revelation in her newspaper column of the lack of competition in WESM may not have automatic evidentiary value before our courts, but it was corroborated, admitted, and exposed by Meralco's own lawyer during oral arguments before the Supreme Court, on the petition for temporary restraining order (TRO) against Meralco's P4.15 per kWh rate increase, as follows:

"Senior Associate Justice Antonio Carpio repeatedly asked how many times Meralco had to buy at P62. (Meralco lawyer Victor) Lazatin stressed no buyer can predict the price; given the mechanics, a buyer only states the quantity it needs and Meralco was a price taker. He further said the 'must offer' rule should cover only power not presold, and the price passed to consumers should be each generator's actual quote instead of the highest accepted price. This, he argued, would make quotes realistic, unlike an extreme zero or P62." (Oscar Franklin Tan, "SC proving wrong place for Meralco case," Philippine Daily Inquirer, February 7, 2014, page A12)

Thus, even Meralco's own lawyer in effect declared that the WESM winning bid rate should be the actual lowest bid price, instead of the highest accepted price, an indirect admission that the P4.15 per kWh Meralco rate increase, corresponding to the WESM winning bid at HIGHEST accepted price, is NOT right, because what is right is the submitted actual LOWEST bid price. And if the P4.15 per kWh rate increase is not right, it should be disapproved on a final basis.

******

I wish government officials concerned in the Duterte administration and in the present 17th Congress would do something about the clearly deceitful and apparently illegal WESM bidding system. Otherwise, this nation is hopeless to poor consumers.

MARCELO L. TECSON
A CPA and Concerned Citizen
C/o San Juan and Associates
27S Midland Manor 2
Ortigas Avenue
Greenhills, San Juan City 1500
8-8-16, 2-12-17, 6-30-17, 7-3-17

2

1st Email: Appeal to All Government Officials Concerned be the Solution Not the Problem, in High Power Rates

Marcelo Tecson
July 15, 2017

To: "Pres. Rodrigo Duterte c/o PACE" <pace_op@malacanang.gov.ph>, all Government Officials and Senators and Official of Energy-related Departments: (same list in previous 4th Email above)

Subject: 1st Email: APPEAL TO ALL GOVERNMENT OFFICIALS CONCERNED: BE THE SOLUTION, NOT THE PROBLEM, IN HIGH POWER RATES
Reply-To: Marcelo Tecson martecson@yahoo.com

The PROBLEM in our abnormally high power rates is not the lack of solutions—because there are some key SOLUTIONS that are doable because their implementation does not need scarce public funds. All that is needed is proper use of GOVERNMENT AUTHORITY.

The PROBLEM in our high power rates is not the profit-maximizing private power companies either, which apparently overprice the power consuming public—including the government as a major power consumer—through unreasonable rates that yield annual returns way above the Supreme-Court ruled 12 percent reasonable limit for public utilities (ERB vs. Meralco, G.R. No. 141314, November 15, 2002, affirmed on April 9, 2003). Profit-hungry power companies cannot do overpricing if the government will not allow it.

The REAL PROBLEM in our high power rates, which serve as obstacle to our economic growth and back-breaking burden to many poor Filipinos, was our past non-performing government officials, who ignored our repeatedly communicated short-term and long-term measures aimed at bringing down our second highest power rates in the region—as can be deduced from the attached copy of our letter to the Ombudsman, which so far has not produced fruitful results.

If the PROBLEM is in our leaders, the SOLUTION is also in them. Therefore, trusting that our present government officials are for real change and improvement of the lives of the now more than 100 million Filipinos, we respectfully endorse to all government officials concerned, for their appropriate action, our herein recommended set of immediate and long-term SOLUTIONS toward power rate reduction.

For your consideration.
MARCELO L. TECSON
RODOLFO JAVELLANA, JR.
A CPA and Concerned Citizen President
Good Governance Advocate United Filipino Consumers
Email: martecson@yahoo.com and Commuters (UFCC)
Email: saveearth_20@yahoo.com
Mobile: 0928 657 5329

Quezon City
2-14,-17, 7-15-17

Cc of 1st to 5th emails through separate letters/emails: Select executive and legislative government officials Select members of media, academe, and economic society Select civil society groups and concerned citizens, etc.

==============

CONTENTS (Abridged)
JUNE 20, 2017 TRANSMITTAL LETTER TO ERC COMMISSIONERS

JUNE 27, 2017 TRANSMITTAL LETTER TO COA COMMISSIONERS

THE FIRST AND FOREMOST DOABLE SOLUTION TO ULTRA HIGHPOWER RATES: ENFORCEMENT OF SUPREME-COURT RULED 12% REASONABLE-RETURN LIMIT FOR MERALCO AND OTHER PUBLIC UTILITES

ANNEXES

A. ACTUAL MERALCO RATES OF RETURN IN 2016 AND PRIOR YEARS SELECT PAGES OF SUPREME COURT DECISION ON 12% RATE-OF-RETURN CEILING FOR MERALCO AND OTHER PUBLIC UTILITIES
B. SAMPLE PAST LETTERS TO ERC COMMISSIONERS ON RECOMMENDED SOLUTIONS TO HIGH POWER-RATES WITHOUT REPLIES OR ACTION

C. SELECT PAGES OF TRANSCRIPT OF ERC HEARING ON APRIL 10, 2017, WHICH REVEALED ERC'S PERFORMANCE-BASED REGULATION (PBR) FORMULA IN COMPLIANCE TO SUPREME COURT DECISION ON CORPORATE INCOME TAX AND 12% PROFIT-RATE LIMIT FOR MERALCO AND OTHER PUBLIC UTILITIES

D. MODEL INDUSTRY REGULATION

E. RORB IS WRONG RATE-OF-RETURN CEILING FOR PUBLIC SERVICE COMPANIES AND SHOULD BE REPLACED BY ROE ADDENDA

F. THE DISGRACE TO LAWYERS AND ECONOMISTS IF ALLOWED TO CONTINUE: FREE-MARKET- COMPETITION HOAX IN WESM

G. HIDDEN MERALCO OVER RECOVERY FROM CURRENCY EXCHANGE RATE ADJUSTMENT (CERA)—WHICH FOR SO LONG HAS ELUDED ERC COMMISSIONERS—SHOULD BE REFUNDED TO UNSUSPECTING VICTIMIZED CONSUMERS

6-21-17, 7-13-17

==============

CONTENTS (Unabridged)

APPEAL TO ALL GOVERNMENT OFFICIALS

CONCERNED

PROLOGUE: EXPOSING THE MYTH OF PRIVATIZATION: CONTRARY TO ITS OBJECTIVE, IT WILL RAISE—NOT REDUCE—PUBLIC SERVICE RATES IN CAPTIVE MARKETS CLOTHED WITH PUBLIC INTEREST

ANNEXES

SOLUTIONS THAT ARE DOABLE BECAUSE IMPLEMENTATION DOES NOT NEED SCARCE FUNDS

1 THE FIRST AND FOREMOST DOABLE SOLUTION TO ULTRA HIGH POWER RATES: ENFORCEMENT OF SUPREME-COURT RULED 12% REASONABLE-RETURN LIMIT FOR MERALCO AND OTHER PUBLIC UTILITIES

2 APPEAL TO GOVERNMENT OFFICIALS CONCERNED TO FREE MINDANAO POWER CONSUMERS FROM UNJUST INCREASE IN GEOTHERMAL POWER RATES FROM P3.00 TO P5.1827 PER KWH

3. THE DISGRACE TO LAWYERS AND ECONOMISTS IF ALLOWED TO CONTINUE: FREE-MARKET- COMPETITION HOAX IN WESM

4. RORB IS WRONG RATE-OF-RETURN CEILING FOR PUBLIC SERVICE COMPANIES AND SHOULD BE REPLACED BY ROE GROSS RISK

MISMANAGEMENT BY PUBLIC UTILITIES

MODEL PRICE REGULATION

HOW TO REDUCE HIGH POWER RATES: OVERHAUL EPIRA—THE CURE WORSE THAN THE DISEASE IN THE POWER INDUSTRY

JUST WHAT IS WRONG WITH EPIRA: WHY DID IT PRODUCE ULTRA HIGH—NOT EXPECTED LOW—POWER RATES?

THE ELUSIVE SOLUTION TO EC ONOMIC STING OR OVERPRICING: RATE-OF-RETURN LIMIT

10. REQUEST FOR INVESTIGATION OF ERC COMMISSIONERS' APPAREN WRONGDOING— AS SHOWN BY KEY INDICATORS OF REGULATORY CAPTURE THAT LEADS TO UNJUST HIGH POWER RATES BACKGROUNDER ON THE WRITER OF ECONOMIC "SACRILEGE"
6-25-17, 7-15-17

NOTE: Select articles on the most clear-cut, pressing, and readily doable solutions are presented in next emails.

3

5th Email: Hidden Meralco Over Recovery From Currency Rate Adjustment (CERA)---which for so long Has Eluded ERC Commissioners---Should be Refunded to Unsuspecting Victimized Consumers

Marcelo Tecson - martecson
Posted Jul 15, 2017

From: Marcelo Tecson <martecson@yahoo.com>

To: "Pres. Rodrigo Duterte c/o PACE" <pace_op@malacanang.gov.ph>, and ALL GOVT OFFICIALS (same list as previous emails)

Reply-To: Marcelo Tecso
martecson@yahoo.com

Backgrounder on Doable Avoidance of Huge Exchange Losses for Needed Protection of Consumers—A Duty of Public Service Monopolies, Bangko Sentral, and Government Regulators Like MWSS, Energy Regulatory Commission (ERC), and Toll Regulatory Board (TRB)

Public service companies, including power distributors like Meralco, partly finance their capital expenditures through foreign loans. Their foreign borrowings, denominated in US dollars or other foreign currencies, are subject to the risk of exchange loss whenever the peso depreciates, which means that the peso equivalent of their foreign loans increases to the extent of the peso depreciation.

To properly address the potential exchange loss, and as part of sound risk management, public service providers should obtain exchange rate hedging on their foreign loans from central bank or other hedging institutions. Exchange rate hedging has different schemes or options, but in general it is an insurance against future exchange losses, under which for the hedging fee payable by the foreign-loan borrower to the hedging institution, the latter commits to sell dollars to the former at scheduled future date at pre-agreed exchange rate. The exchange rate is fixed whether the peso depreciates or not. The borrower's affordable hedging fee is then built into its service rate.

Unfortunately, Bangko Sentral ng Pilipines (BSP), prior approval of which is required for all foreign loans by local borrowers, failed to make mandatory the taking of exchange rate hedging on foreign loans of public service providers in captive markets affected with public interest. It failed to do so despite its being fully cognizant of the crucial importance of exchange rate hedging as safety net against public service companies' staggering exchange losses that are being improperly passed on to consumers and commuters as and when the peso depreciates—as was the case when the peso drastically deteriorated when the old central bank shifted to floating exchange rate for the first time on February 21, 1970.

As our post-EDSA I central bankers—including the highly commended BSP Governor Amando Tetengco, Jr.—have failed to this day to heed the bitter lesson of huge exchange losses from lack of exchange rate hedging on foreign loans in 1970 despite my repeated recommendations to them, without mandatory exchange rate hedging on foreign loans of monopolistic power, water, and toll-road companies, utility and toll-road rates had to be significantly raised after the 1997-1998 Asian crisis owing to consequent staggering exchange losses when the peso permanently depreciated from P26 to $1.00 to roughly P50 to the dollar.

Classic example of avoidable but not avoided drastic rise in service rate from exchange losses was that of Maynilad, which miserably failed to hedge on its $800-million foreign loan assumed from MWSS upon the latter's privatization in 1997. It suddenly collapsed from bankruptcy when MWSS refused to grant its unwarranted petition for huge rate increase (per cubic meter of water) provoked by its roughly P20-billion exchange loss on its West Zone concession area, which was not similarly incurred by Manila Water on its East Zone concession.

Manila Water's lack of similar gargantuan exchange loss on its foreign loan assumed from MWSS—with consequent lack of need for substantial rate increase—was not necessarily owing to its own merit. In reality, it was the direct result of anomalous and lopsided MWSS allocation of spent and unspent foreign loans to the two water concessionaires during the 1997 MWSS privatization: $800 million or roughly 90% to Maynilad and $80 million or about 10% to Manila Water. Maynilad advantageously received $360 million unspent foreign loan (out of its $800-million assumed loan) which it could readily use in its operations. As quid pro quo, it had to disadvantageously assume the much bigger $440 million share of already spent foreign loan—spent or used in previously combined East and West Zones and, therefore, a bigger part of it (not just 10%) should have been equitably allocated further to East Zone based on bigger benefit it received from actual usage of the loan.

Unfortunately, while Maynilad received a disproportionately much bigger allocation of the MWSS foreign loan, with much bigger concession fee payable to MWSS for the repayment of the loan to foreign creditors—which bigger concession fee as part of winning bid rate was the hidden mysterious root of Maynilad's P4.96 winning bid vs. Manila Water's clinching quote of P2.32—it did not know how to protect itself and its customers from exchange losses through highly affordable exchange rate hedging before the Asian currency turmoil. Hence, it collapsed from the weight of its failure to hedge on foreign loan.

Even then, under new ownership and management, Maynilad was able to put one over its millions of water consumers when it successfully underwent rehabilitation and obtained price relief from a regional trial court, which was not the authority and expert on water-rate setting, to begin with.

To resuscitate Maynilad, its new owners petitioned a court for rehabilitation and rate increase. After court hearings where consumers who would pay the rate increase were not consulted let alone impleaded, the court ordered a whopping rate increase of P10.27 per cubic meter in 2005, or more than double the P4.96 per cubic meter Maynilad winning bid in 1997.

Maynilad's P4.96 winning bid was enough to pay its operating expenses as well as concession fee for the $800-million foreign loan it assumed from MWSS at the original P26.00 to $1.00 exchange rate. When Maynilad suffered 100% exchange loss when the peso depreciated from P26 to P52 to the US dollar as a result of the Asian meltdown, granting the same P4.96 winning bid rate to Maynilad for its rehabilitation should be more than enough to take care of the exchange loss. Thus, the cited Maynilad's court-authorized rate increase of P10.27 per cubic meter in 2005 is clearly excessive and devoid of merit. It also made innocent consumers suffer from Maynilad's gross incompetence in not having the foresight and risk-management skill to obtain protective and affordable exchange rate hedging on its huge foreign loan—a one single crucial business decision that spelled survival or disaster for the company.

In the end, Maynilad's monumental failure to voluntarily obtain exchange rate hedging on its gargantuan $800-million foreign loan, as well as Bangko Sentral's gross negligence in not mandating exchange rate hedging as pre-condition to its prior approval of foreign loans by public utilities operating in captive markets clothed with public interest, such as MWSS and Maynilad, resulted in millions of generally poor water consumers permanently shouldering the totally unwarranted whopping rate increase of P10.27 per unit due merely to the fault of Maynilad and Bangko Sentral, the supposed economic and financial experts who should have protected consumers from rate increase caused by exchange losses but did not.

As incontrovertible indicator of excessive court-authorized rate increase and consequent overpricing, three years after the 2005 rate increment, based on its audited financial statements posted to its website, Maynilad earned 247% return on equity (ROE) or capital invested by its stockholders, including foreign investors. In other words, Maynilad's select few "lucky" stockholders earned more than double their actual investment in just one year—a feat rarely achieved anywhere in the world!

Moreover, in the case of Bangko Sentral— with twin mission of price and monetary stability—its puzzling failure to mandate exchange rate hedging on public service monopolies, which consequently incurred unprecedented exchange losses in the Asian crisis, resulted in price increases or inflation in power, water, and toll-road industries. This came to pass despite the presence of highly commended central bankers in Bangko Sentral.

For lack of prior IMF-prescribed exchange rate hedging by Asian corporations with foreign loans, to protect foreign creditors in advanced nations (which control IMF) from impending tsunami of Asian bad loans that would be spawned by Asian currency depreciation from capital flight and currency speculation, with consequent exchange losses, IMF and Asian central banks had to defend Asian currencies from such depreciation through the tight-money policy tool high interest rates, and never mind what would definitely happen to Asian borrowers to be rendered bankrupt and Asian banks to be destabilized by massive bad loans out of catastrophic high lending rates. Despite our touted best central bankers, the Philippines had similar disastrous results because Bangko Sentral obediently and naively followed IMF's fallacious high-interest- rate prescription to superfluous extent, even if it could have resisted for reasons pointed out in ANNEX G-1.

Without Government-Mandated Compulsory Exchange Rate Hedging on Public Service Monopolies' Foreign Loans, Unfortunate Consumers are Again at the Receiving End > of Government Regulators' Lack of Expertise in Regulation, As in the Case of Power and Water Monopolies' Over Recoveries from CERA Which are Not Refunded to Victimized Consumers Owing to Lack of Covering Regulatory Refund Mechanism

In lieu of needed exchange rate hedging where hedging institutions serve as insurers against foreign-loan borrowers' exchange losses from peso depreciation, ERC instituted Foreign Currency Differential Adjustment (FCDA)—duplicated later (with consequent double billing?) then replaced by Currency Exchange Rate Adjustment (CERA)—as power distributors' insurance against exchange losses, with millions of exploited innocent power consumers serving as power companies' insurers or hedging mechanism, without corresponding back-to-back insurance from hedging institutions that will in turn protect them, countless consumers, from negligent power companies' exchange losses. To ERC, it seems it is enough that coddled power companies are protected by consumers from exchange losses. It does not give a damn to potential exchange losses by consumers from exchange-loss risk shifted to them by uncaring ERC and power companies.

Thus, CERA is an unjust and faulty mechanism instituted by ERC for Meralco's recovery of exchange losses on unhedged foreign obligations whenever the peso depreciates in relation to the US dollar. It is adjusted downwards on a prospective basis whenever the peso subsequently appreciates, but ERC does not require retroactive downward adjustment or refund to overcharged consumers for subsequent exchange gain whenever the peso subsequently appreciates, even if such retroactive adjustment or refund is obviously needed, consequently resulting in unrefunded exchange loss over recovery that should be object of Meralco's petition for refund. However, Meralco does not initiate such refund for the unacceptable excuse that there is no enabling ERC resolution for it.

Meralco should have initiated the needed refund through working for the required ERC resolution as part of its responsibility to the public under Section 4 of its franchise, RA No 9209, to "supply electricity to its captive market in the least cost manner."

As part of ERC's regulatory functions under EPIRA, it should similarly initiate the refund through issuing the needed ERC refund resolution if Meralco would not take the first move.

In the absence of ERC regulations on retroactive reckoning CERA over recovery, it is quite evident that Meralco has exchange gain or CERA over recovery which is never refunded to consumers. ANNEXES G-2 to G-2-B show that I myself as Meralco power customer paid CERA charges in 2004, when the peso to dollar exchange rate and corresponding CERA was at P56.267 as shown on ANNEX G-3. As disclosed by ANNEX G-4-A, Meralco has outstanding foreign obligations as of December 31, 2004. Thereafter, the cited ANNEX G-3 shows that the peso appreciated in all subsequent years from 2005 up to 2012, at which last year the peso was P41.192 to the dollar. Meralco wisely paid all of its foreign obligations during the years when the peso appreciated compared to its depreciated level as of 2004, as can be deduced from its CPA-audited financial statements as of 2013, with comparative figures for 2012 (ANNEXES G-5 to G-5-A).

According to ANNEX G-5-A, which formed part of the audited financial statements, all of Meralco's long-term liabilities were denominated in Philippine pesos as of end 2012 and 2013. This can only mean that Meralco's previous long-term foreign obligations, which were also not part of its short-term payables, were paid when the peso subsequently appreciated after 2004. The inescapable conclusion then is that Meralco realized refundable exchange gain, the refund to consumers of which neither Meralco nor ERC initiated to this day. The refundable exchange gain can be substantial. Meralco's external auditor, SGV. should consider disclosing it as contingent liability in its notes to Meralco's audited financial statements, as part of required full disclosure of significant audit findings.

ERC, in turn, should waste no time and issue the needed resolution that will require Meralco to file the needed petition for refund of past CERA over recovery, which should be subjected to proper validation by ERC.

MARCELO L. TECSON
A CPA and Concerned Citizen
C/o San Juan and Associates
27S Midland Manor 2
Ortigas Avenue
Greenhills, San Juan City 1500
July 11, 2017

ooooo

4

Graces – Man's Inhumanity to Man

Jose Ma. Montrelibano
July 20, 2017 – Opinion – Glimpses

"When we do not care, when we who have something or are somebody, do not care, neither will government."

I was first alerted to the existence of a DSWD Center for the Aged in QC a month ago through a Facebook post by Dra. Lorraine Badoy who now serves as Assistant Secretary in the DSWD. This Center for the Aged is named GRACES. I do not know why I find it so grotesque for a center to be called GRACES yet be so criminally uncaring. I wish I could share the pictures of that center, especially of the old and sickly that they host, so a better representation of an ugly truth can be appreciated. Best, though, is for the believers and the unbelieving to visit GRACES.

I As I write this article, I will be using phrases from the first post of Dra. Badoy – without her permission. But I will take the chance anyway. The story she has been sharing is a haunting one that may seem inconsequential in national scene. It is not, though. It strikes at the center of what eats away at our national soul. It hits directly how the poor are devalued, and all the more the sick and neglected among them. By government. By us.

Quoting Dra. Badoy, "Then I went to GRACES – a DSWD Center for the Aged here in QC. And suddenly Jose Fabella Center seemed like a center for excellence. I exaggerate..but not by much.

See this photo? I am so sorry to have to show it to you but in the spirit of TRUTH AS POWER and not turning a blind eye on the tragedies of our fellow human beings, let me tell you what it is.

It is a room in GRACES where one of our senior citizens with a mental disorder has had to live in for years. And if you went there, you'd see cockroaches crawling all over the place—on the walls, on her pile of clothes, on the rotting food. When she is there, cockroaches crawl on her.

That red pail is where she collects her urine. And in that small room is where she defecates. The smell, as you can very well imagine, hits you in the face as soon as you get to striking distance.

I don't need to have this spelled out to me. I know what this is. What this is is NEGLiGENCE. I'm no lawyer, but something tells me we are skating on the thin ice of criminal negligence here— if this were a paying client. But she's poor and all alone so fuck it all. That's the horrific mindset I see here.

I am FULLY cognizant that I am part of government now and that it is the job of government to right this wrong. And we in DSWD are up to it. That we will do all we can—to the best of our abilities—to make sure this injustice is corrected. I burn in shame and pain that it has come to this point."

The pictures she shared tell a worse story than our imagination. I hope she took videos as well. If only to remind us about man's inhumanity to man.

Yes, government is at fault, has been at fault all these decades. And especially government that can waste money on non-essentials like streamers or posters or give-aways when lives are wasted and lost in exchange. And I am not even talking about corruption because I do not want to distract our attention from the painful truth about the value system that we cater to in our society. Yes, government has been at fault; but the greater fault is ours, we who could have done something, not to poor, old, sick and neglected at GRACES, but to all the poor, old, sickly and neglected of our society.

It only begins with caring; or, in this case, it only begins with not caring. When we do not care, when we who have something or are somebody, do not care, neither will government. Because government caters first to those it fears, to those it wants something from. With what is left, government can then consider the poor, the marginalized, who it sees as simple problems that have to be solved or shoved aside. The poor have their great numbers to work with, but they hardly ever count. Except on elections when they are not only problems but serious expenses, too. For numbers to count, the numbers must be together, counted as one – or numbers can be in the tens of millions individually and as powerless individually as well.

Before GRACES, my number one proof of this great collective uncaring by all those who matter in terms of resources and influence was the perpetual hunger of our poor. I had been following the quarterly SWS survey results for more than 15 years and the hunger of 15-20% of Filipinos was being reported faithfully. But for sure, hardly anyone even read, or cared. If we did, that hunger would have disappeared a long time ago. Because there is food, more than enough food – if we cared.

Thankfully, pockets of feeding programs are coming on stream. Somehow, there is a growing realization and concern. This pattern has started and it will continue. It may be starting in poor public schools but it will flow to the streets and under the bridges and the canals. Because more are beginning to care. And hunger will end where caring begins.

It is time to go deeper into the shadows of our uncaring past and let the sunshine through. I know that in GRACES, the first work of cleaning, not just the dilapidated facilities but the bodies of the elderly and sick inside, has started, repairs are being done, and volunteers are responding to the appeal of Dra. Badoy. I know, too, that DSWD is demolishing its old attitude and beginning a fresh initiative from the heart.

Let us join this journey. There is neglect everywhere that hurts and kills our elderly. Let this be the simple change, from uncaring to caring, trigger the great change we have longed for.

Readmore: http://opinion.inquirer.net/10570 8/graces-mans-inhumanity-man#ixzz4nP1QPdWx Follow us: @inquirerdotnet on Twitter | inquirerdotnet on Facebook

ooooo

5

Armageddon

Rey O. Arcilla
July 20,1017 - Malaya

('I told my friend that my considered view is that there is nothing to worry about North Korea or the US launching a nuclear strike against each other any time soon.')

Duterte visits Marawi

My God... I hate corruption! – President Rodrigo Roa Duterte aka Digong.

Now, if only the heads of the other branches of government, the legislative and the judiciary, could also utter the same words with gritted teeth and determination, this country could easily pick itself up from the morass it is in.

Digong has already set the example by giving substance and meaning to his assertion. He has, for instance, fired the DILG secretary and the NIA Administrator, both old friends, and some 90 other government officials for corruption.

Senate President Koko Pimentel, House Speaker Pantaleon Alvarez and Chief Justice Maria Lourdes Sereno should do their part in ridding their respective turf of corruption.

Everyone who cares knows that many honorable members of Congress are still merrily indulging themselves and spending people's money in the process.

Honorable senators and congressmen, for instance, have been going on junkets lately. (Senators going to Paris to "study" climate change?! Congressmen and House staff members, reportedly to be accompanied by Department of Tourism officials, going to Iceland and Norway, perhaps to witness and marvel at the sun that "never" sets in those two countries at this time of the year?!)

Early this year, Senator Panfilo Lacson also insisted that pork barrel, declared illegal by the Supreme Court, has been included in the 2017 national budget.

As to the judiciary, it is common knowledge that some of its members are not immune to corrupt practices.

When will the heads of these agencies begin to follow Digong's example? Needless to say, his efforts to get rid of, if not minimize, corruption also depends significantly on the 7cooperation of these two branches of government.

We can only hope that the officials concerned have as much love for the country and have the same desire as Digong to serve the Filipino people.

SPECIAL ENVOY TO US

An American friend asked me what Digong's appointment of a Special Envoy to the US means.

"Why not a full-fledged ambassador with residence in Washington? Does it mean a downgrading of Philippine relations with the US?" he asked.

I told my friend I could only guess what Digong's reasons might be.

First, he has not found one with the same mindset that he has regarding the form and substance of PH-US relations that are consistent with his decision to pursue a foreign policy that, before his time, was anchored mainly on dependence on the US.

I think he is also waiting for the Trump administration to lay bare its eventual and ultimate policy towards PH-US relations. Right now, Trump is still preoccupied with issues involving Europe, the European Union, Russia, Syria, North Korea and China. These issues, like it or not, are far more pressing and important to Washington at this time.

In the meantime, Trump has decided to adopt a friendly and supportive stance towards Digong by expressing support for what the latter is doing about the drug menace. I suspect though that Trump is simply trying to keep Digong, for the time being, from straying too far from the US fold and falling into the Chinese and Russian embrace.

There is no denying that Digong's independent foreign policy has already borne fruit.

Witness, for instance, the US' more forthcoming and supportive attitude towards us, e.g., her unexpected and sudden delivery of previously withheld arms and ammunition for use by the AFP in ridding Marawi of Muslim terrorists, followed by the USAID announcement that it was delivering aid to the victims of the ongoing conflict.

Note, however, that the US action came in the wake of China's delivery not only of weapons needed by the AFP, but also her immediate contribution of P15 million towards the rehabilitation of the battered city.

Russia, Japan, South Korea and Australia, among others, have also pledged to help in the rehabilitation of Marawi. I have not read or heard of any rich Islamic country pledge assistance.

Here, I would like to quote and thank one "Jaundiced Yellowista" for his/her very succinct comments in one local daily on Digong's foreign policy , to wit:

"Not to put too fine a point on it, both US and China are vying to be on the good graces of Duterte. Even Japan is not far behind. There's just too much geopolitical interest at stake for these countries. They know it, Duterte knows it, and they know that Duterte has the full measure of our country's geostrategic importance to them all. No other president in our nation's history understood geopolitics so well as Duterte does. And no other president played the superpowers with such acumen as Duterte has done. That's also because we now have more choices as opposed to the bipolar world order of the Cold War or the subsequent unipolar world order of Pax Americana. In this day and age of the mutli-polar world order, we got more choices to choose from."

PHOENIX PETROLEUM

A word of thanks is in order to certain private sector companies and businessmen for their ready response to help the people of Marawi.

The latest among these civic-minded entrepreneurs is a friend, Dennis Uy who is president and chief executive officer of Phoenix Petroleum.

Uy announced during the celebration of the tenth anniversary of his company's listing in the PSEI the creation of a P100 million fund he called LIFE, to help soldiers and policemen who were and are fighting in Marawi "secure sustainable livelihood, achieve independence, sustain their families and provide education for their children".

He said businesses should "recognize and assist security forces as they are the ones who make celebrations of milestones of companies possible".

"These times call for a decisive action and a community spirit," he added.

NORTH KOREA

Another American friend asked me what I thought of the North Korean issue.

I gather that many Americans are worried about the issue, principally because of Trump's warning that North Korea could face "some pretty severe" consequences after its defiant test of an intercontinental ballistic missile. They think Trump is "reckless" enough to take such action.

I told my friend that my considered view is that there is nothing to worry about North Korea or the US launching a nuclear strike against each other any time soon.

To begin with, I do not think Trump is that "reckless", especially given the problems he faces at the moment with, among others, China and Russia which are friends of North Korea.

North Korea, on the other hand, will do no such thing without clearance from China. And such clearance is not forthcoming.

I also believe Kim Jung Un knows his country will be obliterated from the face of the earth should he, in a moment of madness perhaps, decide to attack US territory or overseas military facilities.

If that happens, China will be faced with the dilemma of either standing idly by while the US takes retaliatory action against North Korea, or resorting to a military confrontation with the US. In case of the latter scenario, Armageddon would very likely ensue.

I don't think anybody would want that.

Then again, I could be wrong.

MANNY PACQUIAO

Digong was right when he told boxing icon Manny Pacquiao who lost his welterweight crown to Australian Jeff Horn that "weather-weather lang 'yan", which means in Tagalog "pana-panahon lang 'yan".

What Digong meant was that the defeat to Horn was merely a temporary setback.

I take a different view. Pacquiao's "weather" or "panahon" is over. He is already past his prime. He doesn't have the killer punch anymore, as seen in his last few fights, because of Father Time. He should heed the plea of his wife and mother, and the advice of his trainer Freddie Roach to quit now. We do not want to see him end up like Muhammad "The Greatest" Ali, for instance, or some other pugilists who suffered a similar fate.

***

Today is the 81st day of the eleventh year of the enforced disappearance of Jonas Burgos, son of the late press icon and founder of this newspaper.

The family and friends of Jonas hope that the Duterte administration will exert serious efforts to find and haul the perpetrators of Jonas' disappearance to justice.

***

From an internet friend:

Welcome to the Golden Years —

They weren't in my pockets. Suddenly I realized I must have left them in the car. Frantically, I headed for the parking lot.

My husband has scolded me many times for leaving my keys in the car's ignition.

He's afraid that the car could be stolen. As I looked around the parking lot,

I realized he was right. The parking lot was empty. I immediately called the police.

I gave them my location, confessed that I had left my keys in the car, and that it had been stolen.

Then I made the most difficult call of all to my husband: "I left my keys in the car and it's been stolen."

There was a moment of silence. I thought the call had been disconnected, but then I heard his voice. "Are you kidding me?" he barked, "I dropped off!"

Now it was my turn to be silent. Embarrassed, I said, "Well, come and get me."

He retorted, "I will, as soon as I convince this cop that I didn't steal your car!"

***

FB:
https://www.facebook.com/reynaldo.arcilla.9847

Ooooo

6
Cine Teheron and Jerry Lewis

Cesar Lumba
cesar@gmail.com
August 21, 2017

I remember Santa Ana. I remember Cine Teheron. I remember the slapstick comedy of the Three Stooges, then later Dean Martin and Jerry Lewis.

Santa Ana was a small town within the 13.1 square mile city of Manila - a tiny city by any stretch, but a big influence on all our lives. We all lived in that tiny city we called Maynila; not all, some actually lived in Quezon City, Makati City or Pasay City. But most of us lived in Maynila, and we were so happy we lived there.

Some of us who lived in or near Santa Ana could walk to Makati, which still had rice fields where we caught frogs that lived in culverts with our bare hands. We ripped off their legs and roasted those legs on open pits. We scoured the neighborhoods for any signs of those fierce spider warriors that we could put on a stick opposite other spiders who would fight them for meal or survival. We played pantintero and fought other kids who objected to the strength with which we struck their backs as they tried to pass our red lines in a game that pitted escape artists against guards who stood sentry so that no escape artists could pass without being tagged. Gently, according to designers of the game, but hard in actual practice.

A trip to Plaza Lawton was a treat. There was a small restaurant there that served the best ice cream in town. A trip, by the way, that any 13-year-old boy could take by jeepney or bus and his parents would not worry about his safety.

We were street-smart kids.

My best friend in Santa Ana was Willy Gonzales. We met at a Legion of Mary meeting at that time in my life when I was still an openly religious bloke. Willy was in the Legion of Mary because of the girls. He had decided early on that he would be a Catholic because most of the girls in the Protestant church that his parents attended were not as attractive as the Catholic girls he would see walking in their Catholic school uniforms to the local all-girls grade school and high school - the Santa Ana Academy.

Later Willy Gonzales would become my perennial nemesis in chess. He couldn't beat the ones I was beating, but I always found it hard to beat him. He knew my game and capitalized on his knowledge.

Before we discovered chess, Willy and I often went to Cine Teheron. It was that flea-infested theater on Teheron street (a street that has, I think, a different name now) that had wooden seats. The seats were regular theater seats with arm rests and backs, but they were wooden and looked more like benches.

This was the theater where we watched the Three Stooges and the Dean Martin and Jerry Lewis movies. That was the place where I laughed so hard my belly ached. I think the theater charged 25 centavos, or maybe 50 centavos to get in. The movies were worth every centavo we spent.

We watched all the Dean Martin and Jerry Lewis movies shown at Teheron theater - they were still in black and white - and they were the funniest movies I had and have ever watched. Ever - not then, not now.

I assumed that the two would just continue making movies. I never thought the supply would ever run out.

The two were at the pinnacle of their careers and there was jealousy involved. Jealousy always causes breakups.

So no more Dean Martin-Jerry Lewis movies. Jerry Lewis would have a go of it alone, and in color now, but it was not the same. Oh, he still was funny, just not as funny as before, because he did not have Dean Martin as a willing foil.

Dean Martin would disappear all together from the scene, but he would later resurface as a mainstay of the Rat Pack. His role in the Rat Pack? He was still the funny character, the foil. But this time, he had made himself into a cinematic drunk. People loved Dean Martin in his new persona - a funny, sophisticated drunk.

Jerry Lewis, whom most people blamed for the breakup of the Dean Martin-Jerry Lewis tandem, had started to lose his luster. He still made movies, but there was a sense that he had been isolated. And he had lost his mojo.

When Jerry Lewis made his own comeback, which was not really a comeback because he had not completely fallen off the screen, he would become the host and face of the Muscular Dystrophy annual fund-raising campaigns on public television. All told, the fund-raising campaigns have so far raised more than $2 billion. And the generated funds have helped countless victims of Muscular Dystrophy.

Jerry Lewis' passing at age 91 yesterday has struck me hard. He died at 91. I'm 76. Is 15 years the most I can look forward to? Many of us who are in our mid-70s, how long do we have? Jerry Lewis dying at 91 means he had far exceeded his life expectancy at birth. American males have a life expectancy of about 75 at birth. Lewis far exceeded that.

I tell most of my friends that I want to live till the age of 100 or beyond. I think it is doable because I don't have any serious long-term ailments, plus I may have my mother's genes. You see, my mother died at age 101, two months shy of her 102nd birthday.

But even if I last till age 100, that would be just 9 more years than Jerry Lewis lasted. And that's only 24 years from now.

We all will eventually pass away, but the thought of it is scary.

And Jerry Lewis dying is telling us one thing. A part of us has died. Just as Bob Hope dying took something away from all of us. And Frank Sinatra, Dean Martin, Sammy Davis, Jr. dying. And Elvis Presley, Michael Jackson and John Lennon. The list is endless. The list of lost comfort skins that wrapped our lives is ever lengthening.

Many of the institutions in our lives are gone. And they haven't been replaced, can't be replaced. Certainly not by newbies Drake, Sam

Smith, Ed Sheeran, Adele. Those are entertainers that young millennials today will sometimes rue for passing. They can't replace the people who had made us laugh and cry and dream. Mainly because we won't be around when they pass, but also because we cannot recapture the joy we had felt when we were young and we weren't thinking of anything more than what were in front of us, which were the antics of two of the funniest people ever to grace the movie screen.

Jerry Lewis - dead at 91. A part of us is now dead. What remains of us - that we can still use to our advantage. Our dreams, the list of things we still want to accomplish, there's still time. We can have them, achieve them.

Now is the time we 70-somethings must think of ourselves. We must live the lives we imagined because our window of opportunity is fast closing.

I knew I would emulate Danding at least once in my life and this is one of those times I'm doing that by closing with these words:

Love to all,

Ooooo

7

Epicenter of War
Erick San Juan
August 22, 2017

So many issues are noe being thrown at the present administration's ability to handle matters of great concern specifically of drugs and corruption. Campaign promises that has to be curtailed in order to achieve a better life to every Filipino. Are these just lip service after one year in office and there seems to be no major accomplishment?

Yes, these two problems are deeply rooted to the core of the society's socio-political life. Admittedly, past administrations seemed oblivious that such problems existed and the current leadership is painstakingly trying very hard to diminish the effects of such menace.

The entry of huge amount of shabu at the Bureau of Customs vis-à-vis the age-old corruption in the Bureau seems to disregard the marching order of Pres. Rodrigo Duterte to clean this country of drugs and corruption. Accepting the fact that the BOC needs a total overhaul right at its roots to clean the bureau of the mafia within to avoid illegal shipments of contraband. But what about the problem emanating from without?

Pres. Duterte should have realized that transnational shipment of illegal drugs is much harder to curtail than the ones circulating in the country through corrupt politicians and scalawags in uniform. The mere fact that most oppositions (sometimes even pro-PRRD) have been criticizing the present leadership on its soft dealing with China when it comes to the illegal entry of illegal drugs. Obviously most key personalities involved in the illegal trade are Chinese. And so much for all the "palusot" from the Chinese customs on how on earth that hundreds of kilos of smuggled shabu are coming in our ports without their knowledge. Is the Chinese leadership too lax in solving their own drug problem that they also want to export these illegal drugs to us in their favor, economically?

That was my question i asked last saturday at the meeting of Philippine Council for Foreign Relations at Romulo's Restaurant in Bel Air, Makati City from one of the mainland VIP's who attended our meeting as speaker for the China's Council for Foreign Relations. I reiterated to the CCFR group that I know that China's custom is very strict especially with illegal drugs but how come that billions of pesos worth of shabu passes and cleared thru their port and out of the blue, when it entered the Philippine port and delivered, their customs personnel tipped off our customs bureau which led to a bungled operation and non-coordination with our own anti-illegal drugs unit, the PDEA. The rest was history that pressured Commissioner Nick Faeldon to resign.

The Duterte administration should be wary because problems emanating from illegal drugs are going overboard and oppositions are finding ways to use these to destroy and humiliate him. From EJK and human rights violations to police brutality and corruption among "friends" dealing with illegal drugs are easy target to justify a call for a regime change. Even PRD's son is now being dragged into the fray.

Another issue of grave importance is our sovereign rights to our territories that is being challenged again by the Chinese government. The one exposed by Congressman Gary Alejano on the Pag-asa islands.

News reports came out that last week, a Philippine lawmaker, Congressman Gary Alejano, released images showing Chinese coast guard, naval, and civilian vessels within a stone's throw of Pag-asa, or Thitu Island — a significant Philippine possession in the disputed Spratly group of islands.

Pag-asa, which is administered as part of Kalayaan municipality, an archipelagic cluster in the South China Sea.

Shortly after their release, Alejano's allegations regarding the presence of Chinese vessels were independently verified by Gregory Poling of the Center for Strategic and International Studies' Asia Maritime Transparency Initiative (AMTI). AMTI's perusal of satellite imagery acquired on August 13 showed multiple Chinese vessels in the area, including "nine Chinese fishing ships and two naval/law enforcement vessels." A Philippine fishing boat was also docked at a nearby unoccupied sandbar.

The incident remains highly murky, with neither Chinese authorities nor the Philippine government having officially commented on the claims levied by Alejano. Philippine Supreme Court Senior Associate Justice Antonio Carpio described the events underway near Pag-asa as an "invasion of Philippine territory" on Saturday, calling on Philippine Foreign Secretary Alan Cayetano and President Rodrigo Duterte to step in.

One of the features under question in the area is the Sandy Cay. Carpio noted that Sandy Cay, an unoccupied sand bar, "is a Philippine land territory that is being seized (to put it mildly), or being invaded (to put it frankly), by China." (Sandy Cay should not be conflated with the Vietnam-occupied Sand Cay, another feature in the Spratly group.)

Aside from the relatively short list of facts concerning current events — that there are Chinese vessels near Pag-asa Island and both the Philippine and Chinese governments are rather silent about the whole affair — there is little else to be said conclusively at this point. Regardless, whatever is happening, there appears to be a potentially significant change to the status quo in the South China Sea in 2017. We won the arbitration case at the International Court at the Hague but now China is grabbing our islands with consent in the process.

The context of the ongoing Chinese naval and coast guard activity is crucial. First, the Philippines, along with nine other Association of Southeast Asian Nations member states, has just concluded a draft framework on a Code of Conduct for the South China Sea.

Second, it has been less than a year since Duterte visited Beijing, concluding a range of agreements and broadly lowering the geopolitical tensions between Manila and Beijing in the South China Sea — tensions that appeared to have reached their apotheosis last year as a Hague-based arbitral tribunal ruled almost completely in the Philippines' favor in a major case concerning maritime entitlements and other issues in the Spratly group.

Beyond the context and the facts, however, analysts are left mostly to speculate about possible Chinese intentions and the factors governing the Philippine government's remarkable silence about an unusually broad Chinese presence near Pag-asa.

Instead, Duterte has said that the Chinese are there to "patrol" since "we are friends.

"China assured me that they will not build anything there. I called the Ambassador, I said, when I read – (They said) 'We will assure you that we are not building anywhere there,'" the Philippine president added. The assurances were reportedly delivered by Chinese Ambassador to the Philippines Zhao Jianhua and the Chinese Foreign Ministry.

Duterte's remarks on Monday raised more questions than answer. If there was an existing understanding, why did neither the foreign secretary nor the minister of defense issue clarifications early last week? Second, did Duterte order Philippine Navy vessels to stand down from the area and allow the Chinese Coast Guard and People's Liberation Army-Navy access to the waters near Pag-asa and Thitu Island? Finally, how does the president explain reports of Philippine fishing vessels being denied access to the waters if these are indeed friendly patrols?

Given the legal stakes involving Sandy Cay highlighted above, the Duterte government's nonchalance about ongoing Chinese activities at Pag-asa remains unconvincing. Perhaps the Philippine government will soon offer a more compelling rationale for the ongoing activities, before it's too late. (Source: Ankit Panda, August 22, 2017)

I hope that Pres. Duterte will soon realize that he's being perceived by critics as a 'China doll' willing to be a governor-general of Philippine Islands, Province of China. As the saying goes, 'Only fools don't change their mind.' PRD was believed to be a socialist bit his change of heart with the left could also happen despite China's ongoing salamization of our country. He has to act fast before we become the epicenter of a looming war between the US and China.

Leave a living legacy Mr, President!

Ooooo

8

Father's Little Pagan

Elisa Guerrero Yogore
Dateline: April 6, 1956
Weekly Woman's Magazine, Philippines

A MAN TO REMEMBER

The good Father wanted to be sure it was not only for the convenience of the family that this Protestant wanted to be a Catholic.

To measure a man's true worth, it has been wisely said, look not at what he has achieved for himself but at what he has done for others. By this criterion the late Fr. John P. Delaney, S.J., was a great man. In the short span of 40 years that he walked the earth, he did a lot of good for a lot of people—people who, now that he is dead are only too glad to tell their stories so that his revered memory may be perpetuated. From time to time, WWM will publish a first-person account of one individual's experience with the late priest. WWM wants its readers to be multiplied a thousand fold and that, in death he may (reach) the many people he had so desperately wanted to reach in (life).

ONE DAY it dawned on me: my kids are growing up, but they didn't even know a single prayer. And the situation struck me as incongruous because, as the daughter of a protestant minister, I have been raised to regard religion as a very important thing. But my husband was Catholic, and our children had been baptized in the Catholic Church. And there was the rub.

As their mother, it was my duty to teach them their prayers, but how could I teach them about something which I knew nothing about, something which I did not believe in? It was up to my husband, therefore, but he couldn't do very much. First he was in the United States studying to be a better doctor. Then, when he came back, he was so busy in his work as a parasitologist that he hardly had any time for his family.

Being a trained nurse by profession, I had long ago learned that when one has a problem, the best thing to do is to ask a specialist to help solve that problem. So I went to a specialist.

And that was how I first met Fr. John P. Delaney of the Society of Jesus.

I had, of course heard of him. I was a member of the Diliman community and my Catholic friends had told me of the wonderful work he was doing as chaplain and spiritual advisor of U.P. students and faculty members. I went to him with some misgivings, fully expecting him to bulldoze me into becoming a catholic or , that failing, to ignore me completely but I was wrong.

Patiently, quietly, he listened to my problem. In the end he gave me a little book of prayers. "This will do for a start," he said. "Drop by now and then to tell me how you are doing."

I did that and in one of my periodic visits, I brought my husband with me. He and Father Delaney hit it right of from the start-- well. And (then) with my husband insisting that the Yogore family be included in the list of Dilimanites who at least once a month, played host to Father Delaney at breakfast, lunch or supper. (The good father, it will be remembered, never did any housekeeping in the hole-in-the-wall he used for quarters. He had all his meals with his parishioners.)

The arrangement suited me fine. He wasn't a finicky eater—as a matter of fact, all of us complained that he never seemed to eat enough—and it wasn't any trouble having him for a guest. And my children were crazy about him. They would clamber all over him. All of them fighting for the privilege of sitting on his lap. He always seemed to have a stock of funny stories to tell them.

But, though I along with my family began to look forward to his monthly visits, a thought kept nagging at me. Before very long, I told myself, he will ask me to become a Catholic. At any moment now, he will tell me to give up my faith and join his fold.

But not once, in a word and action, did he broach the subject. He talked of most anything but matters of faith. He asked my children how they were doing in school, he engaged in long conversations about my husband's work in malaria control, he talked to me about child care and such other housewifely subjects, but never did he discuss religion.

And as the months passed one thing stood out. My husband, who heretofore been like most men in the discharge of their religious duties, had lost his lukewarm attitude and become a more conscientious Catholic. I was very happy about it, needless to say.

But my husband's renewed zeal posed a new set of problems. On Sundays, when we all set out for church, we parted company somewhere along the way, I to worship at the Protestant chapel, he and the kids to hear Mass in the Catholic chapel. And the children began asking questions, questions whose answers they were too young to understand. Questions like, "Why does Mommy not come with us to church? Why is she always going away somewhere?"

To stop the questions, I took to hearing Mass with them—and attending Protestant services later in the day.

Things were at this state when my husband was given another fellowship to the United States. He could not have chosen a worse time to leave. I was on the family way and my conception was particularly difficult. I was miserable and in pain all the time. He was reluctant about going, but I finally persuaded him to take the offer since he should not pass up the chance of a lifetime.

One of the last persons he saw before his departure was Father Delaney. "Look after my family, Father," he told him. "I will feel much better if I knew you were taking care of them." Father Delaney promised.

And he lived up to that promise. He stepped up his visits to us. Quite often he would drop by, unannounced. "I want some coffee," he would tell me, "make me some." And, though I was wallowing in self-pity and misery since I was conceiving and my husband was not with me, I had to get up and make the coffee.

LOOKING BACK, now, I can see that he had a purpose in doing this. He wanted me to stop feeling sorry for myself by keeping me busy. He was a very wise man. Very solicitous, too, since he was always asking us if we needed anything, if he could be of some help in one way or another.

My misery, however, was not due exclusively to the child I was carrying in me. There was something else, I was tortured by the realization that because of my different faith, my family would always remain divided, that it would never know the complete togetherness, the unquestioning unity and solidarity welding most families so compactly. While there was a cleavage in religion, there would always be disharmony somewhere else.

In adhering so steadfastly to my Protestant persuasion, was I being selfish? Was I depriving my family of the happiness of true unity by my stubborn stand? Wouldn't everything be much simpler if I just became a Catholic?

So, one day I went to him. "Receive me into your church, Father." I told him, "I want to be a Catholic."

But he saw through me immediately. And his answer was no. "One doesn't become a Catholic for convenience, child," he said gently. "One must be intellectually convinced that Catholicism is the true religion. "

"Then convince me, Father," I said desperately, urgently. But again his answer was no. Instead, he gave me some books to read. "Those will tell you something about the faith you think you want to embrace," he said.

So I read the books. And whenever he dropped in to see how the kids and I were doing, I always plied him with questions. Always, he answered the questions as well as he could, dispelling whatever lingering doubts were in me. But always, he never discussed religion unless I asked him to.

As all this was going on, I stopped completely all my church-going activities both in the Catholic and in the Protestant chapels. I figured that I could not arrive at a fair—to myself, my family and everybody else—decision unless I effected a sort of religious vacuum first. It was during this time that Father Delaney took to addressing me as "my little pagan."

AFTER SEVERAL MONTHS of this, I was ready to become a Catholic. And I asked to be baptized. But again, Father Delaney was firm. The answer was still no. Not yet, anyway. I was lonely, he said in effect, and I missed my husband a great deal. Because I missed him so, it was possible that I might be thinking about him and seeing him in a new, unrealistic light. Maybe I glamorized him, maybe even his religion seemed glamorous to me. Maybe that was why I yearned so desperately to embrace it.

"At least, let us wait until he comes back," he said. "Then, you can look at things in their proper perspective."

I admit now that I could not understand his attitude. The way I saw it, he should have been very glad to convert me. Wasn't that, after all, his primary mission as a priest? But he didn't operate that way.

Disappointedly, I went back home and settled for a long wait. As the days passed, the conviction that I wanted to be a catholic not only for spiritual but also for intellectual reasons continued to grow in me. In one of my letters to my husband, I wrote: "When you come back, I hope to take a step which will make us all very happy."

IN SEPTEMBER of last year, my husband returned. If Father Delaney expected my religious fervor to diminish in the ecstasy of reunion--was disappointed. But again, he did not volunteer to baptize me. He was content to wait.

He did not have to wait long. About a month after my husband's return I went to hi again. And again, I asked him to baptize me. He took one look at my face and he said earnestly, huskily, "Yes. This afternoon."

That afternoon, in a chapel somewhere in Grace Park, I was received into the Catholic Church. And early the next morning, I received for the first time as a Catholic the Body and Blood of Christ through the sacrament of the Holy Eucharist. I have been receiving Him every day since.

Barely two months afterwards, Father Delany died. I was among thousands who mourned his passing. As he had done with the thousands who like me attended his funeral, he had enriched my life, given it a purpose. More important, he had left me a priceless legacy: the legacy of salvation of peace of mind, of happiness. No man can give more than that.

ooooo

9
Kill-Pa-More Administration? The Tagubas.

Rene Saguisag
Dateline, August 24, 2017
Manila Times Opinion

What should come out tom, another potpourri/medley

* Kian delos Santos was well, just 17, if you know what I mean, and the way he looked, was way beyond compare. Very very dead he was. *

* No, we are not reprising the Beatles.*

* It is not in the national interest, in my view, to pressure Prez Digong to quit, given his overwhelming mandate last year. He must succeed. He must not fail. Else, we all lose. *

* It is however in the national interest to pressure him to abandon his failed, bloody, messy anti-poor drug policy which has not succeeded anywhere. *

* The short and simple annals of the poor matter. *

* No matter Kian's background, his seeming rub-out looks indefensible. As was the case of Ka Lando Olalia and his driver, Leonor Alay-Ay, in 1986, apparently done in by RAM (Rebolusyonaryong Alyansang Makabansa) leaders we met in 1985, when we were much younger and

fresher; it was not about money but a better nation we furtively broke bread for.*

* In our old age, RAM now reportedly seeks amnesty with back pay from Digong, with his well-known soft spot for the police and the military. Fine, but what about Ka Lando and his driver, murdered so cruelly? Ka Lando's mouth was wide open when found, grimacing in pain.*

* RAM met with Digong and may get what it wants - amnesty and back pay - in a Kill-Pa-More administration. Another hedge against coups?*

* RAM never staged a single successful coup. In February 1986, the People rescued the trapped group from being barbecued in their failed coup attempt. Cardinal Sin and Butz Aquino asked the people to support and rescue RAM, helpless, retreating, not attacking. Entire families were at EDSA, asking what they could do for the country.*

* A bright shining moment. *

* Now, RAM asks what the country could do for them. *

* Just turned 78, I know how it is to be ageing and ailing. Hospitalization and medicine and professional charges are costly so I try to be understanding. But, what about Ka Lando and his driver? (Not to mention the civilians arrogant RAM killed just for showing support for duly-constituted authority?) *

* It was on November 13, 1986, when Kilusang Mayo Uno (KMU) leader Lando and his driver were found in Antipolo. Their bodies had been mutilated beyond recognition. A scar on Ka Lando's leg was the only mark that confirmed his identity. *

* The NBI, in its report to Prez Cory in 1986, said the killings were a prelude to "God Save the

Queen," a supposed coup plot by RAM to rid the Aquino Cabinet of left-leaning members. *

* In January 1998, the Department of Justice (DOJ) filed a case as a new witness, former T/Sgt. Medardo Dumlao Barreto came forward, implicating several RAM leaders in the surveillance and abduction of the victims. Barreto said he surfaced out of fear as several military men who had known about the murders were ordered killed or mysteriously died. Dead men tell no tales. (But, for Kian there is CCTV, today, as well as brave live eyewitnesses.)*

* In May 1998, a five-man DOJ panel filed two separate cases of murder against 13 RAM members in the Antipolo Regional Trial Court. Among those charged were retired Colonels Eduardo "Red" Kapunan and Oscar "Tirso" Legaspi, a fellow Bedan. (Another fellow Bedan, Labor Minister Bobbit Sanchez, the original MABINI chair, had left the country on a tip, and survived, unlike Ka Lando.) *

* Red and Tirso sought immunity from prosecution, arguing that Proc. No. 347 granted by FVR to rebel soldiers "extinguished their criminal liability." They said political assassinations, such as the Olalia-Alay-ay double murder case, could have been part of simulated events intended to create an unstable situation favorable for a coup. In 2009, the Supreme Court dismissed their petition and ordered the filing of murder charges.*

* In February 2012, the Antipolo City Regional Trial Court issued arrest warrants against thirteen defendants. On July 24, Perez surrendered and later pled "not guilty" to the murder charges. The two cases are now pending in Taytay. *

* I have no objection to amnestying RAM, which did its invaluable part in ousting Macoy, but a measure of justice is also owed Ka Lando, et al..*

* A cussing Kill-Pa-More President and a sadistic RAM aren't, and do not represent, what we are as a people.*

* Last August 21, there was another gathering of millennials (and "perennials," added one who looked like Reli German). Our hairline and ranks are thinning and many have gone to a better place, with no shoddy and bloody police operations.*

* Last Tuesday, for instance, I heard from Philip Suzara of the April 6 Liberation Movement that, Ed Olaguer, of the Light-A-Fire Movement, aided by courageous heroes Al Yuchengco and Mon Diaz, is gone. Condolences. Philip is a first cousin of Jinky Suzara, who married Gary Lewis, a son of iconic Jerry Lewis, a fave in our youth, also gone. Jerry made us laugh while Digong makes us cry, in the human rights sector, and now, elsewhere *

* Digong should stop scaring human rights advocates - we aren't his enemies - even if long ago, we mastered the art of pretending not to be afraid.*

* That is one lesson he should have learned by now. We leave everything to the Lord and can pretend to be unafraid. *

* I am not now for ousting him but he must change and show some respect for the human rights to life and dignity.*

* Ninoy belonged to the elite, scared and angered by what happened on August 21, 1983. When we in the opposition met in the home of Esto and Maur Lichauco on August 7, 1983, we all looked

forward to August 21. All save a Rand expert who said Ninoy would be killed at the airport, instead of being taken back to a prison cell. Naaah, Macoy wasn't that stupid. I would openly concede then that he was a criminal genius. Back to Fort Bonifacio, we said. *

* We asked Tita or Dona Aurora what she thought and she said she agreed with the think tank expert, her son would be killed at the airport. Huh, why Tita? She said, "kutob ng ina." *

* Anyway, because of the salvaging, I got to meet courageous Mrs. Soledad Duterte, Digong's Mom, who was among those who led the Yellow Friday movement in Davao City, for Justice for Aquino Justice for All (JAJA). *

* Where is the elite today? Just another day in the office, absent the economic crisis of 1983-86? Where is Makati Business? The Integrated/Inutil(?) Bar of the Philippines? The Philconsa?*

* Meantime, the Senate in a bipartisan move quickly caucused on EJKs. The House? Silent. BTW, has some Senator asked if Mark Taguba, a San Beda Alabang grade school alum, is related to famed Fil-Am U.S. Maj. Gen. Antonio Taguba who reported on military abuse in the Al Ghraib prison? Whistle blowing is in the blood? I have asked my studes to trace the connection, if any, the surname not being common. (I had a law stude nicknamed Taguba, Class '66, who migrated to the U.S., where we met decades ago.)*

* Anyway, for-from-elitist Kian, yagit. has done us the favor of stopping Kill-Pa-More, for now at least. Seemingly. And of making Digong stop saying "I have your back." But, he has no business talking of the guilt or anyone, not of the

cops', not of Sen. Leila's, given the powerful effect of presidential rhetoric on human conduct. Just say "follow the evidence and let the system work."*

* One Caloocan prosecutor fell all over himself making sipsip, lawyered for the cops, saying what he thought the unpredictable Digong had wanted to hear. Nabuking. Belat.*

* When Prez Nixon condemned Charles Manson, et al., for the grisly slaying of Sharon Tate, et al., Tricky Dick got hammered all over. The White House quickly apologized and said Nixon had not meant to prejudge anyone. See Vincent Bugliosi's Helter Skelter.*

* Here the cops and Leila cannot expect a fair hearing. Mistrial, I fear, which could lead to dismissal, assuming fear and ambition would not get in the way. The load is heavy enough without a madaldal Prez interloping, encroaching and intruding.*

--

Saguisag & Associates Lawyers 4045 Bigasan Street, Palanan 1235 Makati Office Nos. (+632) 551-6350 <+63%202% 20551%206350> /833-4140 Fax No. (+632) 831-2276

ooooo

10
Think Out of the Box
Erick San Juan
August 30, 2017

We are now a nation being challenged once more with several issues emanating from the present administration's policies concerning its war on drugs and corruption. The latest word wars among government officials - appointed and elected has created more problems than solutions.

Filipino people are fed up with such bickering and endless "he said, she said" rhetoric in the midst of high prices of commodities and utilities that affects the daily life of an ordinary Juan dela Cruz. Pundits are asking," Where are the promises pertaining to a better life for every Filipino especially the poor?" Even the middle class families are slowly inching towards the lower class status.

Are we seeing a repeat of the past administration's promises that were never fulfilled that has created the hardships we have today? Particularly, the supposed positive economic results of foreign investments. Is it still the same 'old trickle-down effect' or all B.S. and just taking this country for a ride?

News of investments that will bring jobs via build, build, build seems to be trapped in the drawing board yet. Or the observation of some analysts that we are being herded (like a herd of cattle) into a debt trap. Which is which? Are we really moving towards industrialization? Meaning more jobs – more buying power for the needy and more opportunities for growth?

There seems to be a problem, to some geopolitical experts on our relationship with China – economically. More skeptics are saying that we are being pushed towards a debt trap which we are not aware of due to the 'friendly ties' that PRRD used with China, a.k.a. soft power on the part of China. And on the occasion of the launching of the so-called One Belt, One Road (OBOR op) operation initiated by China, it was assessed by some geopolitical-economists that we will be used as dumping grounds of manufactured goods from China. Translation – the true economy of China lies on its manufacturing which seems to be overheated and they have to unload these somewhere and it is a win-win solution to recover from their economic downturn.

China is not giving away money or goods to be used in infrastructure via the OBOR op, there are 'soft loans' and maybe some geopolitical maneuverings on the leadership of countries, especially claimants in the contested areas who joined in the OBOR.

Of course when data/statistics that are sourced from Chinese-controlled sites – it's all rosy and healthy economy, but the big questions is: is it the true picture? Or just 'fake news', as the trending word nowadays?

From the words of Mehreen Khan – "The true state of China's economic fortunes remain a mystery to the world. The latest round of official quarterly GDP statistics from Beijing' s National Statistics Bureau show the economy has slowed to its lowest level in 25 years. Quarterly growth is at its lowest rate since the depths of the financial crisis six years ago.

Yet the government's estimates have long been dismissed as an accurate barometer of what's really going on in the Chinese economy.

"There has been a long history in China of the official GDP data understating true GDP during a boom and overstating it during a slowdown", wrote Willem Buiter in September- a former Bank of England rate-setter and influential economist at Citi.

Questions over China's "actual" rate of growth have been thrown into sharp relief after a summer of turmoil in financial markets. Sudden anxiety over a Chinese "hard-landing; left investors dumbstruck. Billions were wiped off global stock indices and authorities were forced to suspend trading to prop up equity prices.

China data-watching has now become the main driver for global economic sentiment."

I will not dwell into technicalities here, our country should be more concern on how President Rody Duterte and his so called economists handle the crisis once the huge red dragon will hit the bottom, and unfortunately, we will go down with it. Are we prepared? Or some will say – it is better to wage war and fight that outside enemy to save China's internal crisis. But still, who will be minding the store once it hit us?

Possibly Pres. Duterte can feel the heat this time. Our peso is on a freefall, high prices of commodities was compromised by bird flu hype, infestation, the month long Marawi siege, the shocking control of top chinese drug lords of our political system and possibly behind terrorism to weaken our nation. That even the Marcoses are even attempting to dupe him of the fools gold and stale gold certificates to avert the global class suit the Marcoses will face soon. Pres. Duterte was even advised by some vested interests to implement a revolutionary government which will surely fail time due to the infighting from within including his political party mates. The president should think and act out of the box if he wants to survive this crisis by design.

ooooo

11

My Family's Memory of the Magsaysays

Rodel J. Ramos
August 31, 2017, Facebook

Senator Ramon Magsaysay junior's visit to Toronto revived pleasant memories of the Magsaysay family. The boy we called Uniong (he hated this name very much) is now a Senator. Everybody had native weird nicknames then. Jun's father, the late President Ramon **Magsaysay was Monching, kuya Jess was Susie, Dad was Kikoy, and close friends and relatives know me as Rudy. During my Dad's time, when the Magsaysays visited Zambales even after Tio Monching became President, they always drop by and sometimes slept over at our house. The difference was, while they came as a family before becoming President, they now brought with them a bunch of guys which later became the famous like Sen. Manuel Manahan who run for President under the Progressive Party, later the Grand Alliance, Ex-Senator Raul Manglapus, Mayor Antonio Villegas, and others. When we were in Manila, we also stayed in their house in Singalong and later in Malacanang.**

My late brother Jess Ramos stayed with the Magsaysays at their Singalong house while studying in Ateneo de Manila. Jun Magsaysay was in De La Salle College. Our families were so close that we called the late President Tio Monching and his wife Tia Luz. Old people say that the Magsaysays are related to the Ramoses of Zambales, but we did not bother to trace it. When I got married, Tia Luz became our Ninang with Mila Magsaysay as her proxy and so with Tio Jesus Magsaysay. We lost contact with them after the death of Tio Monching. I was a student activist during my college days and it was the norm to hate the rich and powerful. We believed then that they were the cause of poverty and all the problems of the nation. I avoided influential relatives and friends and hated to go to them. So when Jun Magsaysay came to Toronto with his lovely wife and brother in law, I met him in the Airport with Consul General Francisco Santos. He asked me if I was the youngest son of Tio Kikoy because I looked like my father.

Realizing that you need influence to progress in the Philippines, I asked for an appointment with Jun Magsaysay with the help of my Compadre Ex-Mayor Pito Garcia of San Antonio, Zambales. Jun just came from Malacanang and President Fidel Ramos just gave his blessings to run in his ticket as Senator. I was one of the first to know. In fact he showed me the book autographed by the President. He treated us to lunch in Quezon City Aristocrat Restaurant. The late President Ramon Magsaysay was the best friend of my father, Francisco Ramos of San Narciso, Zambales. They were classmates in Zambales Academy in San Narciso.

They parted ways when my Dad went to Munoz Agricultural School and Monching studied commerce in Manila.

They were reunited in Try-Tran Bus Co. owned by the late Teodoro Yangco, the philanthropist. Tio Monching was the Manager while Dad was the chief mechanic. When the Japanese invaded the Philippines in 1942, they both formed the Western Luzon Guerrilla Forces in Zambales, later known as the Merrill Guerrilla and then the

Magsaysay Guerrilla Forces. Tio Monching became Commander with the code name Chow, Dad as the Chief of the Intelligence. His code name was Ram. Dad also organized the movement in the towns of San Antonio, San Narciso, San Felipe, Botolan, Iba, and Palawig. When the Japanese found out that Ram was my father, all his parents, sisters and brothers were rounded up, incarcerated and threatened with execution if Dad did not surrender. Dad panicked and was on his way to give himself up in Fort Santiago. Tio Monching catch up with him in a caritela in Santa Mesa at a stormy night and pleaded with him not to surrender. His life and the lives of all the guerrilla members whom he kept the roster were in danger. Fortunately, he was convinced. His family was later saved by a Japanese woman we use to call Nana Masay married to an Almazan who convinced the Japanese that this family was law abiding. In return, the Ramoses never charged the Almazans electricity bills while she was alive because they owned the Ramos Electric Co. of San Narciso. My lola Petrona Tadena Ramos died later out of fear during those agonizing days.

After the war, Dad got busy running his Nepa Soft Drink Factory and selling rice mills and tractors under International Harvester while Magsaysay started his career in politics and run as Congressman of Zambales. It was in the last days of this campaign, during a motorcade rally that we first saw the popularity and charisma of this man destined to become the most loved President of the Philippines, the Man of the Masses. We expected only a few hundred to join the rally. The motorcade was from one end of town of San Antonio to our town San Narciso. The sad part was, it was 2 o'clock in the afternoon and the people were very hungry when they stopped by our place. My parents only prepared sandwiches and soft drinks for hundreds, but there must be 10,000 people there. And they came down and took every bottle of soft drinks we had in the Factory. And we never got back the bottles. During those times, the soft drink was only P0.10 but the bottle cost P1.00 each.

This started the trouble for my Dad, and he never recovered from this financial losses. He had to borrow money from the RFC to buy extra bottles. Ramon kept on telling Dad that his Guerrilla back pay will pay for this debt, but it came too late.

When Magsaysay became president, people were telling my Dad to ask help from the president, but he had the pride not to ask his friend a favor. He always said, "When he needed help, he came to me. He should know when I am in trouble and come to me." But a president has the troubles of the entire nation to fix and would not know what is happening to his closest friends. But my father's troubles finally became known to the president, and he send a cable to Dad asking him to come to Manila. He offered him the position of Chief Inspector of the Graft ridden Board of Liquidator. Their generation was the incorruptible bunch and no matter how many bribes were made to Dad, he would not take them. When Magsaysay died, the people of President Carlos Garcia asked him to "Roll your mat." in other words resign, so that they can do their dirty work once more. And Dad founded and led the Progressive Party in Zambales and joined with the Magsaysay group. They won in Zambales and Metro Manila but lost in most of the Islands. During those days, the birds and the beast voted and so with the dead in the cemeteries especially in Mindanao.

During these campaigns, another Magsaysay was trained by my Dad in politics. Manong Tony Diaz whose mother was a Magsaysay always joined the campaign of my Dad in the Progressive Party of the Philippines (PPP) and later Grand Alliance. Antonio Diaz became the Congressman of Zambales, while Vic Magsaysay is the Governor. My brother Jess Ramos became the speech writer and secretary of Vic Magsaysay and Governor Amore Deloso at certain times.

Magsaysay remembered

Rodel J. Ramos

I remembered that day Tio Monching died very well. My Dad, Francisco Ramos was one of the best friends of

Tio Monching. March 17 was the fiesta of St. Joseph which is the Patron Saint of Quirino District, Quezon City where we use to live.

My Dad was not able to sleep that night and at 3 o'clock dressed up and went to my sister's house which was half a mile away. My sister asked what my Dad was doing at 3 o'clock in the morning at their place. He said, he was restless and could not sleep.

We were all busy preparing for the fiesta that morning and several visitors were already there when the news on the radio came that the RP Mt. Pinatubo, the President's airplane was lost. My Dad started crying because he was sure Tio Monching was dead. He had that feeling. And so did my Mom. We did not enjoy that fiesta nor did our many visitors that day.

I don't know when they found the plane crash, but only Nestor Mata survived the tragedy and told the story. There were speculations that it was a CIA plot because Magsaysay was so popular and was then resisting the demands of America. Some say it was the making of Vice Pres. Carlos Garcia's people who stood to benefit from his death. There were rumors that Tio Monching was alive as was being cared by Aetas in the wilderness of Cebu. It was a day of mourning for the whole nation. He was the most loved president of the Philippines. The line ups of people from Malacanang to his grave in La Loma were never seen before and you can see the tears in the eyes of all our people.

Magsaysay came and went like a comet in the dark of night in Philippine history. He stopped the growth of Communism with the surrender of Luis Taruc and the capture of Jesus Lava, his brother and Pomeroy. In Mindanao, the Muslim leader Kamloon also surrendered. It was the only time the Philippines experienced peace as a nation but was short lived. Luis Taruc and Kamloon felt the sincerity of Ramon Magsaysay and his love for the poor. When Governor Montano of Cavite did not want to give up his private army, he led a battalion to Cavite to force him to surrender.

Honesty was his trademark. He loved the poor people and his charisma was so great. He minimized corruption. Some of his famous quote was: "If my father is corrupt, I will send him to jail." "He who has less in life must have more in law."

I was yet a child when he came and sometimes sleeps in our place in San Narciso. I saw him as a common man, joking, eating and drinking with my Dad and some other friends. I do believe that great men are ordinary people driven by great desires and motivated to achieve great things in life.

Ooooo

12
Hitler's 'Sieg Heil'; Immunity

Rene Saguisag
August 30, 2017,
Manila Times Opinion

Prez Digong making the clenched fist gesture with visiting Aussie spymaster Nick Warner was embarrassingly reminiscent of what Hitler's troopers would do. For our Prez to sandbag a guest to do Hitler's infamous "sieg heil" gesture with him is insensitive. Flak would follow. I agree that the gesture seems "entirely inappropriate" . The gesture is illegal in Germany. But dis is d Pilipins? *

It may bespeak our ignorance of its Hitlerian provenance or our gross insensitivity. It reminds us of the MARCOS! HITLER! DIKTADOR! TUTA chant of the Dark Years.

I don't know if the middle and upper classes really feel safer today. I doubt that the masses do, given the anti-poor thrust of failed drug campaigns. Can one imagine Tokhang and house-to-house drug testing in unique Forbes Park? Only in our countless Pobres Parks are these inflicted.

The death certificate of Kian may state as cause of death: Duterte' s Anti-Poor program, which at the least occasioned, if not caused, his demise. On whose hands is the blood?*

So much needless divisive anger and enmity in a non-healing presidency. Sabong in the Supreme Court. Sabong in the Comelec. A seeming catfight between PAO and a Senate member. Also PAO versus NBI. Also the Ombudsman? They are co-workers in government?

Non-lawyer presidential spokesperson Ernesto Abella says trust the system, a sea change from what lawyers Duterte, Aguirre, Calida and Panelo do, condemning personalities critical of the Prez.

Digong met Kian's parents. Good. He is Prez of all the people.

But why make them do "sieg heil?" Then he sends Chief Inspector Jovie Espenido to Iloilo City whose Mayor is said to be in some narco-list. Why not simply prosecute him, if the State really has the evidence? Iloilo City Mayor Jed Patrick Mabilog is in no hurry to go to the Promised Land — or where his foes tell him to go. He is vocal, not silent, about wanting to see the Prez so he can sleep again. As it is he is seen or misperceived as a Dead Man Walking, with a death warrant. Jovie may yet be remembered as a new Jovito Palparan or Rolando Abadilla, seen as butcherss.

A suspect in a stationhouse is reminded that he has the right to remain silent, a human and constitutional right seemingly checked at the Senate door in the Kian investigation, among other probes. The Senate Committee on Public Order and Drugs is supposed to probe in aid of legislation. Yet, we have well-meaning Sen. Manny Pacquiao saying to a cop: "If you don't talk when the public here is watching, you'll really be seen as guilty." He should have shown some respect for the Bill of Rights. Senators are sworn to uphold it, a document of distrust in powerful governors, and should correct, not enhance, misperceptions.

Even a rookie cop Mirandizes a suspect in custody: "You have the right to remain silent, etc.," showing due regard for the Bill of Rights, so disrespected in the House and Senate, which should work out immunity before making a guest become the tool of his own damnation. Else, they are like Torquemadas of the Inquisition, doing the best thinking and practice of the middle ages.

Under U.S. federal law, which may guide us here, Congress may work for immunity to witnesses who testify at congressional hearings, following a certain procedure. If two-thirds of the members of a committee vote to grant it, a request goes to a federal judge, who must issue an order granting immunity. Once granted, nothing the witness says can be used in a criminal prosecution against him.

Congress itself cannot grant immunity in the U.S.

There, Congressional staff will typically talk with the Justice Department before deciding what to do. And before granting immunity,

Congress will insist on knowing what the witness would say, which is usually in the form of a written proffer. Staff will first coordinate with the prospective resource person, which common sense dictates, but is not done here. There is a rush to grandstand, preen and torment.

I trained in Arnold & Porter and know a bit about such routine prior coordination. I would attend Senate hearings in the U.S. Congress as a water boy of sorts assisting senior counsel, such as Joe Califano (he had three secretaries - including a Miss Connecticut – and he later became a Cabinet Member in the Carter administration**). The courtesy and dignity "all around won't ever be beyond easy recall".

Why the need for immunity? Because without it, a witness in the U.S. can refuse to answer questions citing the Fifth Amendment protection against self-incrimination. Once immunity is granted, the witness must answer. But, the U.S. Congress rarely grants immunity. The last time was 2007, when a Justice Department aide was called to testify about the firings of U.S. attorneys, I am told by Fil-Am lawyer Chuck Medel.

Our wild probes, so directionless and insensitive, drove two guests to suicide.

We speak above of procedural due process. For substantive due process, Uber paid a humongous fine of P190M - for conveniencing the public? On what legally tenable, intellectually respectable and psychologically satisfying basis? But, moot and academic as Uber has paid. No Uber-da-bakod multa po sana, ha? No payment under protest for a test case?

Anyway, Digong has no known or ballyhooed program to alleviate our traffic woes, now worse than ever. He just does not talk about it. No way out? We may have to agree that always telling the truth may not work or be advisable if we are to maintain relationships in the real world, says Nick Hornby in Fever Pitch. You don't tell a mother about the appearance of a baby with a face only she could love. Be kind.

On truth telling, Comelec chief Andy Bautista supposedly lied in his SALN. R.A. No. 3019 and R.A. No. 6713 coexist. There is a report that someone in Mindanao has been charged by the Ombudsman with violating both. I am not privy to the details but some years ago, the Commission on Civil Service, if memory serves, decided to change its format to add what Sec. 7 of the Tolentino Law requires of a public servant, to include ". . . a statement of the amount and sources of his income, the amounts and sources of his income, the amounts of his personal and family expenses and the amount of income taxes paid for the next preceding calendar year." A good clause. I doubt that Andy Bautista has complied. Indeed, is anyone among our 1,600,000 civil servants in compliance?

Year after year I challenge my stude to show me a form showing compliance by anyone. No one has been able to, despite the promise to pass on that feat alone. I bet Digong does not comply with said excerpt from Sec. 7 (but complies with Sec. 8 of the Salonga Law I sponsored and defended on the floor). I have a copy of his SALN. He names some seven kin in government but does not state who is an asset and who is a liability.

Before charging anyone for violating Sec. 8, the public servant concerned must be given a fair chance to correct and tell the truth. My/our intent was to punish recalcitrance. The law is more administrative than punitive. But, our law made jobless Chief Justice Rene Corona, a post-midnight appointee named on May 17, 2010. GMA was supposed to be just a caretaker then; a new Prez had been elected.

Indeed the ban on midnight appointments starts two months before the election. Antedating seems to happen however so that a new Constitution should say only appointments made and published before the interdicted period would be valid, to plug a loophole in the 1987 Constitution which speaks incidentally about ill-gotten wealth.

Digong said an emissary of the Marcoses offered to return their loot in the billions with some gold bars to boot. We are told however that for every five things he says, to take seriously only two, with three for the comic page. Criminal genius, I have often said of Macoy, which could spread in the family by osmosis or descent. I am incredulous, as I write.

Let us see if we have front page (40%) or comic page (60%) stuff here. Statesman? Or comedian? Anyway, we again chant, "nakaw na yaman, ibalik sa bayan."

The Marcoses may be the last ones to know, as it were, but trust Digong to make things happen.

"Ma'am, kahiyaan na po ito, labi ni Sir, I'm under pressure to return to Batac, sabi ni Mamagawin ko po."

The Art of the Sandbag.

And The Deal. Libingan.

Saguisag & Associates Lawyers 4045 Bigasan Street, Palanan 1235 Makati Office Nos. (+632) 551-6350/833-4140 Fax No. (+632) 831-2276

ooooo

13

Andres Bautista: A Reflection of the Philippine Elite's Dysfunctionl Relationship with Society

Allen Gaborro
September 1, 2017, Yahoogroup

Allow me to preface this piece by stating that I am the first cousin of Patricia Bautista, the estranged wife of Philippine Commission on Elections (COMELEC) chief Andres Bautista. Although we are cousins, Patricia and I have not been in touch for several years now although this is not due to any acrimony between us. As fate would have it, we simply drifted apart over the years as can unfortunately happen to familial relations, particularly when they have resided half a world away from each other for most of their lives.

The fact that Patricia and I are related as first cousins could cause some to question the objectivity of what I have written below. Indeed, some could mistake me for being prejudiced by my blood connection to Patricia for I express views that I will admit, are sympathetic to her and critical of her husband. All I can say to that is, each reader will have to decide for themselves how much they are willing to take to heart and mind from what I have written. If readers cast doubt on my words because of my relation to Patricia Bautista then let that be their conclusion.

But I happen to believe that everything I have written here has suffered the wrath of my desire to always speak truth to power. The ideal reader should look for reason and logic in my comments and observations and not for glaring lapses of sentimentality for a beleaguered relation. For what it's worth, I am supporting Patricia's audacious—if arguably self-serving—move as something that is most certainly in the best interests of the Filipino nation.

****

I have to say that I'm not entirely surprised by the revelations of alleged corruption on the part of Comelec Chairman Andres Bautista. Rumors of his suspected financial malpractice—not to mention the hearsay on what has been described to me as his "compulsive" marital infidelities—have made the rounds over the past few years.

But merely discussing and spreading the rumors about Andres amounted to not much more than the dissemination of unsubstantiated *tsimis*. In other words, it was always intriguing to talk about the corruption and infidelity speculation, but there was never anything resembling hard evidence to prove either one. That is until now, what with the stunning discovery of suspicious financial documents by Andres's wife, Patricia (Tisha), in their conjugal home.

Upon hearing the jaw-dropping news, I communicated my support to Tisha by way of Facebook. I told her that I was behind her one-hundred percent in coming forth in front of the media. In the presence of her interviewers, Tisha appeared composed and persuasive enough to convincingly raise the specter of her husband's financial malfeasance.

Conversely, I knew her skeptics would question Tisha's motives as they called to mind how tangled and contentious her marriage settlement negotiations with Andy had gotten. Some thought Tisha's gambit to be a maneuver to extract a fortune from Andy who claimed he had no such fortune. This is an oversimplification in light of everything that has happened.

Whatever her motives were, Tisha did the right thing. She put her well-being, and conceivably her physical safety, on the line by verbally highlighting glaring details of her husband's purportedly illicit activity. Tisha's decision goes to show that what I believe is Andy Bautista's arrogance, perhaps as much as the corruption allegations now besetting him, is what has him in hot water right now. It is a good bet that he never expected his outwardly soft-spoken and mild-mannered wife to rat him out. Ironically, Andy's smugness in regards to what he expected of his wife has made all the difference in upending and potentially destroying his professional life and his individual freedom.

One might surmise this arrogance stems from what could be an old-school Filipino attitude on the part of Andy, an attitude about marriage that bestows upon the husband the carte blanche to engage in any sort of sordid escapade he desires while the wife is consigned to the position of the silent, acquiescent bystander.

Having met and conversed with Andy a few times in the past, I was always struck by what I perceived to be his paradoxical disposition: he never failed to display an easy, down-to-earth temperament. But at the same time he evinced a subtle sense of conceit, an allusive air of superiority to anyone he was talking to. After taking these observations into account, we can deconstruct them and discover for ourselves how like a proverbial Machiavellian politician, Andy Bautista has worked his respectable public image so as to shroud the shadier reality behind it.

In a wider context, the Bautista scandal calls attention to the ongoing, dysfunctional relationship that the political and economic elites have had with the rest of Philippine society. Instead of unity and cooperation between the classes, the elite and their equally amoral, hypocritical lackeys—a deplorable list of sycophants and parasites that may include Andres Bautista—have devalued the legacy of national solidarity and consensus that was realized during EDSA I in 1986.

The lofty vision of the AmBisyon Natin 2040 public plan states that by 2040, "the Philippines shall be a prosperous, predominantly middle-class society where no one is poor." However, the way things are looking right now—especially under the murderous Duterte administration—that vision is more likely to be dashed as a result of the unremitting errors of judgment and failure of leadership on the part of the political and economic elite.

The legal predicament Andy Bautista finds himself in is just one of the latest illustrations of the top-heavy modern structure of corruption, cronyism, and criminality that has crowned Philippine politics and economy since the advent of American colonialism at the turn of the 20th century. Keeping that in mind, the dogged pursuit of justice in the case of Andres Bautista provides no guarantee that it will be served.

But for the millions of Filipinos who have experienced enough shame, guilt, and anger at the hands of the elite in almost complete anonymity, the process of bringing about lasting social justice, empowerment, and accountability in their country will get a huge lift by making sure that with Andres Bautista, any inexcusable misdeeds are dealt with firmly and fairly.

Oooo

14
Milestones
Chapter 1: EDSA 1
Revolution

Larry Henares
February 23, 1996
Article - Make My Day Book -12
Fire and Fury

Part 1. Our EDSA changed the world!

During World War II, during the Japanese Occupation and on the eve of Philippine Independence from the United States, there were only 13 democracies in the whole world. By early 1970's there were 44 democracies in the world and the Philippines under Marcos was not one of them. Many newly independent former colonies and emerging communist regimes became authoritarian, and outnumbered the democracies, 66 to 44.

Then the EDSA Revolution happened. The Cable News Network or CNN came into being, and satellite communications became commonplace. For the first time in history, one mass movement riveted the attention of the world.

Hour by hour for four unforgettable days, on satellite television the world over, people watched the events unfold in the Philippines as they happened, with the Filipino message to its own people and to the world -- that a peaceful revolution to end armed authoritarian rule is possible if the people are united and determined -- that the human spirit is unconquerable, resilient, and potent against the forces that seek to destroy it.

"Why not us?" asked the Poles, the East Germans, the Czechs, the Chinese and the Romanians, and others. And in the wake of Edsa, 45 countries or one third of the countries on this earth decided to transform their political systems. From 44 democracies in 1970's, by 1991 the number doubled to 89 democracies, probably the greatest expansion of freedom in history! And for the first time democracies outnumbered authoritarian regimes two to one.

Today we celebrate the tenth anniversary of the EDSA revolution and its impact on the rest of the world: First, EDSA in 1986 inspired and accelerated the fall of the Communist world through people power in Eastern Europe. In Hungary elections in

1988. In Poland the electoral victory of Lech Walensa against the Communists. In East Germany, the crumbling of the Berlin Wall in 1989, and the reunification of the Germanys in 1990. In Czechoslovakia in 1989, Vaclav Havel becomes president of a multi-party congress. In Romania in 1989, Ceausescu's Communist government is overthrown. In 1990 Yeltsin is elected president of Russia, in 1991 the Soviet Union is dissolved.

Second, traditionally government by autocratic governments at least five Latin American countries choose to have democratic governments: In Haiti in 1986, dictator Baby Doc Duvalier is overthrown and flees, in 1991, a priest is elected president. In Chile in 1988 a plebiscite rejects dictator Pinochet, and a Christian democrat is elected president in 1989. In Argentina free elections in 1989. In Brazil, in 1989 the first popular election in 28 years. In Nicaragua in 1990, free elections depose the Communists and elect a woman to the presidency.

Third in Asia, Pakistan in 1988 elects a woman president against a military regime. Also in Myanmar in 1990, a woman president is elected, placed under house arrest, and is awarded the Nobel Peace Prize., In Turkey in 1990, the first woman prime minister comes to power. In South Korea, democratic forces comes into being peacefully. And South Africa gets rid of apartheid in 1991 and elects a black president in 1994

Part 2. Our EDSA accelerated the fall of Communism

The term People Power was born on EDSA in 1986. Why not us? asked the people behind the

Iron Curtain and in a dramatic turn of events, the Cold War between the United States and the Soviet Union ended.

1) In 1988, in Hungary, Kádár was replaced as party leader by a moderate reformer. In 1990 the conservative Hungarian Democratic Forum (HDF) and its allies won a parliamentary majority. József Antall became prime minister, and Árpád Göncz, a writer and former dissident, was elected president. The new government embarked on the privatization of Hungary's state enterprises, selling interests in more than half of such businesses by 1993.

2) In 1989, in Poland. the Communist government agreed to legalize the Solidarity union and reorganize the parliament and presidency. In limited free elections, Solidarity-supported candidates won (1989) nearly all the seats they contested. The parliament narrowly reelected Jaruzelski president, and he offered the premiership to Tadeusz Mazowiecki of Solidarity. Mazowiecki initiated a transition to a free-market economy, which brought economic hardship and disruption. In 1990 Walesa became president, defeating Mazowiecki in a free election. In 1991, parliamentary elections gave 29 parties seats. Hanna Suchocka became Poland's first woman premier in 1992, but she lost a no-confidence vote the next year. In new elections the Democratic Left Alliance (former Communists) and Polish Peasant party (PPP) together won a majority, and Waldemar Pawlak, of the PPP, became (1993) premier.

3) In 1989, in East Germany came the downfall of Chancellor Honicker. The Berlin Wall crumbled in October 1989, and in October 1990, eventually the two Germanys were re-united.

4)   In the wake of the "Velvet Revolution of Prague", in December 1989, for the first time the Czechoslovakian Parliament elected a multi-party congress, and the new president, the poet playwright Vaclav Havel, in his visit to the Philippines, acknowledged his country's debt to EDSA.

5) From 1965 to 1989, Romania was ruled by Nicolae Ceausescu. He reduced the country to poverty to pay for a radical program of modernization. In Dec. 1989 antigovernment violence broke out in TimiSoara and spread to other cities. Army units joined the uprising and Ceausescu fled, but he was captured, tried, and executed. The National Salvation Front, headed by Ion Iliescu, subsequently won (1990) an election and became president.

6) In 1990 in a free election, Boris Yeltsin won as President of Russian Federation. In August 1991, an attempt to have a coup d'etat to oust Gorbachev as Soviet First Secretary failed because Yeltsin supported Gorbachev. Finally, in December 1991, the USSR was dissolved and was transformed into the Commonwealth of Independent States in December 1991.

Part 3.   EDSA inspired five Latin American countries to democratize

The effect of EDSA on the authoritarian regimes of Latin American is just as impressive. In the 1980s, the democratization of Ecuador, Peru, Bolivia, Uruguay, Honduras, El Salvador, Guatemala and Grenada antedated the EDSA Revolution. Traditionally governed by corrupt and cruel military regimes, the Latin peoples of at least five countries were inspired by EDSA to mount their own people power movement to cast off their yokes.

1)   HAITI: In 1957 François "Papa Doc" DUVALIER was elected president. Supported by a personal police force, the Tontons Macoutes, he imposed an especially repressive rule, relaxed to some degree only after his death (1971), when he was succeeded by his son, Jean-Claude Duvalier, about the time Marcos seized power in the Philippines. "Baby Doc" fled the country in 1986 a few days after Cory came into power, and a period of social and political unrest followed. In 1991 Jean-Bertrand Aristide, a popular priest, became president after free elections; the army ousted him later that year. The Organization of American States called for his restoration and imposed an economic embargo, but a series of civilian leaders were appointed while the army retained real power. The UN approved an oil (1993) and near-total trade (1994) embargo and subsequently authorized the use of force to restore Aristide. In 1994 an agreement calling for Aristide's return was negotiated amid invasion preparations by the U.S., and U.S. and Carribean forces oversaw Aristide's restoration to power (Oct. 1994).

2) CHILE. In 1973 following Marcos' declaration of Martial Law with US support, in Chile a U.S.-supported, bloody military coup resulted in the murder of President Salvador Allende. A repressive military junta, headed by Gen. Augusto Pinochet backstopped by an Opus Dei group headed by Pablo Baraona, governed from 1973 to 1990. After EDSA, a 1988 plebiscite rejected Pinochet's bid to remain in office another eight years. Patricio Aylwin Azócar, a Christian Democrat heading a coalition of

17 center and left parties, won the presidency in 1989, but under the military-drafted constitution, Pinochet remained head of the army. Eduardo Frei Ruiz-Tagle, the son of Allende's predecessor and a Christian Democrat, became president in 1994.

3) ARGENTINA. After its defeat in the Falklands War with Great Britain, the Argentine military government fell into disrepute. Free elections were held in 1989, and a civilian Carlos Saúl Menem, was elected president. Menem reduced the government's regulation of the economy, privatized state-owned enterprises, and introduced austerity measures to control persistent inflation.

4) BRAZIL. In Brazil, in 1989, in the first popular election in 29 years, Fernando Collor de Mello won the presidency. Collor's presidency was marred by corruption, and he was impeached in 1992 and resigned. Vice Pres. Itamar Augusto Franco became president.

5) NICARAGUA. In 1990 a free democratic presidential election resulted in the unexpected defeat of the autocratic Communist regime of Daniel Ortega by a woman opposition candidate Violeta Barrios de Chamorro, and the Sandinista government and the contras agreed to a cease-fire.

Part 4. In Asia, our EDSA brought three women leaders to power

In Asia, the effect of EDSA was not only to usher in people power, but also promoted the ascendancy of women leaders in nations traditionally male dominated. Actually Asia gave us our first women leaders even before EDSA: Madame Sirimavo Bandanaraike of Sri-Lanka, Golde Meir of Israel, and Indira Gandhi of India. But these three came into power legitimately. The Asian women leaders who came after them, became heads of state against authoritarian regimes on the crest of popular will and people's power.

1) PAKISTAN: In 1977 Gen. Muhammad Zia ul-Haq deposed President Bhutto and later (1979) hanged. Zia died in a suspicious plane crash in 1988. A few months later the opposition Pakistan People's party won a parliamentary majority, and its leader, Benazir Bhutto, daughter of Zulfikar Ali Bhutto, became prime minister and the first female leader of a Muslim country. In 1990 Pres. Ghulam Ishaq Khan dismissed Bhutto, charging corruption and mismanagement. In new elections her party lost its majority, and Nawaz Sharif became head of a coalition government. When he moved to reduce presidential power, he was dismissed (1993) by Ishaq Khan, precipitating a crisis that led to the resignations of both Sharif and Ishaq Khan. Bhutto's party won the most seats in new elections, and she became prime minister of a coalition government. Farooq Leghari, a Bhutto ally, was elected president.

2) MYANMAR (Burma). In Sept. 1988 the military brutally crushed prodemocracy demonstrations and took direct control of the government, but later promised national elections. The antigovernment National League for Democracy, whose leader, Aung San Suu Kyi, was under house arrest, won the 1990 parliamentary elections, but the military refused to surrender power and continued to suppress opposition. Aung San Suu Kyi is the first woman prime minister in a country ruled by a military clique. Placed under house arrest, she fought for freedom and democracy. She eventually received

the Nobel Prize for peace. Her present fate is unknown.

3) TURKEY: Parliamentary elections in 1991 ousted Özal's Motherland party from government and shifted power to the new prime minister, Süleyman Demiral, of the conservative True Path party. Pres. Özal died in 1993 and was succeeded by Demirel, and Tansu Çiller became prime minister. Tansu Ciller was elected as the first woman prime minister of the once powerful Ottoman Empire now Republic of Turkey. the first woman ever to hold that post.

4) SOUTH KOREA. In 1992 Kim Young Sam, a former opposition leader who had merged his party with Roh's, was elected president, becoming the first civilian to hold the office since the Korean War. South Korean's Cardinal Kim and opposition leader Kim Dae Jung acknowledged the inspiration of the Edsa Revolution in their struggle for democracy. After he saw Jaime Cardinal Sin play a pivotal role in the downfall of Marcos, Cardinal Kim called for democracy and constitutional change in Korea for the first time. Said Kin Dae Jung, opposition leader: "They succeeded in the Philippines, and maybe we will succeed here. This is the time of people's power in the developing countries of Asia. We have never been so sure before."

Part 5. In 1898, in 1946, in 1986 we Filipinos showed the way for the world!

In 1898, the Philippines under President Emilio Aguinaldo executed the first nationalist revolution in Asia, and set up the first democratic republic in all of Asia. In 1946, with the restoration of its independence from the United States, the

Philippines is the first colony to achieve independence from the colonial powers, and started a wave of independence movements that liberated most of the colonies of the West, notably Indonesia, India and Pakistan in Asia, and the most of the Western colonies in Africa, the West Indies and Indochina. It is significant that the EDSA Revolution of 1986 inspired many countries to cast off the yoke of authoritarianism, such that for the first time in world history democratic governments outnumbered authoritarian regimes, and at the ratio of two to one.

The EDSA revolution was not an authentic revolution like the French or Russian Revolutions, in the sense of a mass supported seizure of political power to transform the social order. It is definitely a revolution to restore a pre-martial law elite democracy, transferring conservative power from one oligarchy to another, backed by the military. But it inspired genuine revolutions all over the world.

Aside from the fall of Berlin Wall and the Communist authoritarian regime, the most important aftermath of EDSA was the dismantling of the white racist regime in South Africa. F.W. de Klerk, who became president in 1989, removed the ban on the black party, African National Congress (ANC) and other anti-apartheid parties and released Nelson Mandela and other political prisoners. All remaining apartheid laws were repealed in 1991, and an interim constitution ending white rule was completed in 1993.   A multiparty transitional government council was formed, and the first elections open to all races were held in April 1994. The ANC won over 60% of the vote, and Mandela was elected president.

Writing of EDSA and its aftermath, Francis Fukuyama in his famous article, "The End of History," underscored the failure of strong governments of the Left and the Right, and argued that "liberal democracy may constitute the end point of mankind's ideological evolution and as such constitute the end of history."

Such is the legacy of our EDSA Revolution to the rest of the world.

February 23 to 29, 1996, ISYU

Ooooo

15
Midnight at Orangeburg

Julia Carreon-Lagoc
Sept. 7, 2017,
Accents

Could there be a midnight at high noon? Yes, and I'm affirming this with a calm, cool and collected "I-witness" account in any court of law. It happened on August 21, 2017—significantly printed 8.21.17 on the T-shirt that I bought in Orangeburg, a city in South Carolina—a most memorable State in the U.S. of A., at least to me.

The day before, David, my daughter Randy's better-half, searched for the best site in the whole of America with which to view the total solar eclipse. The result: Orangeburg, a three-hour drive from their residence in Bluffton, South Carolina. The specific place: South Carolina State University where we were one of the families that converged in the huge University Stadium.

A souvenir that I still have in my desk is the spectacle labeled ECLIPSE SHADES, given free to all who came for the great event. Now I have all the time to read what's written at the back of the specs: "INSTRUCTIONS FOR USE: Wear your Eclipse Shades to protect your eyes from solar radiation any time you look at the Sun or the Sun's reflection. When looking at a solar eclipse, use your Eclipse Shades whenever ANY PART of the Sun, no matter how small is visible. This product should not be used with any other optical appliances such as cameras, telescopes or binoculars. This product is not a toy. Children should use only with adult supervision." On the other side of the specs is a "WARNING: NEVER LOOK AT THE SUN WITHOUT SPECIAL EYE PROTECTION. DO NOT USE IF DAMAGED. Using damaged Eclipse Shades can result in severe eye injury. BEFORE EACH USE: Check front and back of each lens for damage such as scratches, pinholes or separation from frames. If damaged, cut into small pieces and discard. DO NOT attempt to clean or disinfect. (Under general conditions of use, this should not be necessary)."

Why do I write all these here? Because my daughter Randy said that in 2042, the total solar eclipse will be viewed in our part of the globe, the Philippines. You may check her findings. To be knowledgeable is to be prepared. Knowledge is power, goes the cliché. But where will I be in 2042? I will be 106 years old by that time. Will this centenarian still have the breath of life by then? Or, I'm already up there in high heavens in the company of my dear departed Rudy, a human rights lawyer. Prior to the climactic moment, a gigantic white balloon was hoisted in the middle of the University

Stadium — untied to soar up high, getting smaller and smaller until it disappeared from our sight. It was a weather balloon in a science experiment related to the eclipse. The Emcee had a resounding command of the ceremonies which included the University's marching band that prepped up the audience. And there was the Professor (I failed to get her name) who briefed us on the forthcoming mesmerizing wonder of the Universe that, thankfully, Science can explain. In the ancient past, children were foolishly told that the Sun and the Moon were engaged in a wedding — "A Tale Told by an Idiot" if I have to mock via Shakespeare. To the Scientists, bravo for throwing superstitions, prognostications, and the like into the garbage bin.

The clouds gave way as the Sun ever so slowly went into the shape of a crescent. From the heat of high noon, the atmosphere grew cooler and cooler, the Stadium lights dimmer and dimmer. There was hushed silence. Finally, the totality of it all, and never more was the audience rapt in unity. On that very day, it was most fitting that I wore my favorite green T-shirt boldly blaring the words: ONE LOVE—ONE CHANCE—ONE WORLD—ONE EARTH.

In the span of the night sky, we saw the planets Mercury and Venus predominant in the tiny glitter of stars. My granddaughter Danika, who dreams to be an astrophysicist, shed tears in sheer amazement. That midnight at Orangeburg was an experience of a lifetime. juliaclagoc@yahoo.com

Julia Carreon-Lagoc was a columnist of PANAY NEWS for two decades. She pops up with Accents now and then.

ooooo

16
Retrieving Grandmothering

Julia Carreon-Lagoc
Sept. 10, 2017
Accents

California, USA—In computer lingo, what you are about to read is a retrieval. A favorite columnist in the San Francisco Chronicle has a name for the columns he reprints: he calls them a classic. What I'm retrieving may not be in league with what he calls a classic, but it sure is handy when one is out on vacation and loving it. Sept. 11, the second Sunday of September 2016, is Grandparents' Day, and what I have from the archives is—in computerese—a retrieval. Read on:

This is about a grandmother of some 30-odd grandchildren gifted by her 3 daughters and 4 sons. Gifts, she called them, her word of preference. She died at age 86 and must be well above and beyond a hundred years old were she alive today. Dolores Calantas-Rivera was my grandmother lovingly remembered by this granddaughter every Grandparents' Day.

I myself am a grandmother of 4 grandkids — 1 in native terra firma and 3 on this side of the globe. I'm not writing about me as a grandmother. I leave the scorecard—the pluses and minuses—for the grandkids to fill up as I journey on to my own grandmotherhood. It is but right.

What I am to a great extent, I owe to Lola Loling, some of whose habits, beliefs, likes and dislikes I imbibed through my mother. First page in my book of remembrances was that Lola was not a believer of superstitions. I've always believed that Lola was born ahead of her time. In that age when other grandmothers won't allow using the broomstick at night, she would tell us to sweep clean the mess under the meal table. The belief then was that whatever fortune you possess will be swept away in the dark when you use the broomstick at night.

While many others would wait for the morning before separating from their pesos to pay out debts, Lola was the type to make good her money obligations any hour of the night. "Magbayad ka sang utang mo para maka-tulog sang ma-ayo." (Pay your debts in order to have a sound sleep). The same readiness to pay for debts she expected from some poor folks in the community who would go to Lola for financial difficulties.

Talking about debts and debtors, I remember Lola to have a bad word for usurers — money lenders "nga naga-puga sang balhas sang mamumugon" (squeezing the perspiration out of the workingman). Lola understood micro-finance as early as in the 1940s and '50s. She would have been happy today to know how micro-financing benefits the little man without having to run to "5-6" bloodsuckers.

Lola had her way of going against traditions. At the day and age when the practice was to wear black for one whole year to mourn the passing away of a close relative, Lola defied the custom. Not in outward appearance do you show your grief over the death of a loved one; what counts is what is in the heart. I could almost hear Lola asserting that in crisp

Ilonggo. I lost my mother ahead of Lola. Nanay died of breast cancer at age 56. Before the one-year mourning was over, I was pregnant with my second child and wearing black was very inconvenient as the black outfit absorbed much heat. Lola said to stop wearing black if doing so was uncomfortable. Wear what's convenient was the advice. Yes, dear Grandma, it's not the outward appearance that matters; what counts is what one feels in the heart.

Where's the chink in the armor of this formidable woman? Others may not consider this a weakness, but I consider it a flaw in her person: being a habitual smoker of the dobla (rolled tobacco). The strong tobacco leaves must have contributed to bouts of asthma that finally did her in. All her three daughters didn't take after her smoking. Neither did us, her granddaughters, except one residing in Manila.

I deplore the fact that Lola was a "pangging-gi" (card game) addict. After every lunch, she would prepare the pang-ginggi table for her friends. Only one of her three daughters followed her footstep on this aspect of her life. But she didn't go nuts over the popular game of chance—the "daily double" or jueteng—then rampant in the whole town. Lola must have realized how jueteng siphoned off money from the townspeople.

Lola was a wide reader. Using a "kingki" (gaslight in a recycled bottle), she would read late into the night the Hiligaynon and Yuhum, the two popular vernacular magazines of her time. She made clippings of her favorite novels. Voracious reading was one aspect of her life I inherited, and which I abused. How? I would readily pick up a book to avoid household chores. Lola would tell Nanay,

"Pabay-i ang bata kay nagatu-on." (Leave the child alone because she is studying.) Lola must have seen through the ploy, but she left well enough alone.

The nicest thing about Lola was that she was not a nagger, not your typical grand matriarch on the ready to spill out grandmotherhood statements over and over. I could never remember having been nagged by my grandmother. Credit that to the one writing here being a good grandchild (conceited?), or just knowing when to stay away from creeping sermon time.

One memorable picture clearly etched in my mind was the picture of Lola, misty-eyed, as she looked at the gracefully curved, concrete staircase—the one remaining relic of her and Lolo's mansion-like abode—being dug out of its foundation to give way to the construction of a grandson's house. With a teardrop, Lola accepted how the old passeth away to give way to the next generation. Lola remains an incandescent light in the distant past, just as she had made of her daughter Cristeta Rivera-Carreon—my very own mother—forever aglow in the heart.

* * *

Being a columnist of this paper has given me a chance to sing paeans to my grandmother. Send me your own best memories and we'll see about getting them into print. juliaclagoc@yahoo.com

Ooooo

17

Mother - a sweet word to utter

Julia Carreo Lagoc
May 11, 2017
Accents

Down memory lane, this sterling gold of a tribute radiates with love and inspiration. Read on:

Mother's Day is celebrated every second Sunday of May, and one celebration that the years have not erased in my mind's eye is the picture of my youngest daughter Raileen, then in the grades. She was on the school program to deliver a tribute to mothers. Hers was a childlike yet booming voice as she opened her piece: "MOTHER - what a sweet word to utter!"

Who is to refute the sweetness of that word? Neither you nor I except the unfortunate ones who must have suffered from a psychological trauma vis-à-vis mothers. Nonetheless, theirs are entirely different stories for psychiatrists to unravel and to cure.

Is there ever a politician's wife who has a distaste for politics? That would be a rare breed. Count my mother, Cristeta Calantas Rivera before her family name became a hyphenated Rivera-Carreon. She was apolitical in every sense of the word—an exception in our political landscape where wives are hell-bent to tussle for their husbands' victory or to install themselves as heir apparent or replacement to the "throne" when the incumbent's term has expired.

Nanay wanted Tatay, Simplicio Cordova Carreon, Sr., to continue being the high school principal rather than follow the urgings of friends and relatives that eventually installed him Oton mayor for three terms. Oh well, the rest is history, to use a convenient phrase.

In the whole length of father's political life, I never saw my mother campaign for my father. I think her being kind to everyone was her strongest force to win people to vote for her husband. Never have I heard her speak ill of other candidates nor of another human being. And never ever have I heard her say a cuss word in all the years that she had nurtured us all seven children. Gosh, it is as if I'm on a campaign binge for my mother with this column. No siree! Like my Mom, I harbor strong aversion to the murky world of politics that has gone to the dogs, reeking with redolent wheeling and dealing. In landing a job, often it is whom you know instead of what you know. My apologies to the straightforward ones who stand unshaken on their merits and irreproachable character.

Of the many jeep rides I took from school to home, I recall one instance where I was exchanging views with a fellow passenger. Someone beside me remarked: "Now I know why you are good-natured (yes, me!). It's because you are the daughter of Titang (fond name for my Mom)." A compliment more in praise of my mother rather than this writer. What did I say to that? "Sa kamalingking (small finger) lang ako ni Nanay." The Visayan idiom of self-deprecating comparison had hit its mark.

Mother possessed a compassionate nature I could not equal. She tended a sari-sari store, and she kept a box containing a long list of debtors because she said she just could not refuse a person in need. She would limit the goods a person needed from her store, but turn him away, she couldn't. When she succumbed to breast cancer at the prime age of 56, the whole barrio mourned her passing. When we sent her to her final resting place, a long line of barrio folks joined the funeral procession. An aunt commented, "I wonder how many of those people have unpaid goods from her tiangge (mini grocery store), how many are in her list of debtors."

Mother was the epitome of cool. How I would have wanted to inherit her composure in confronting "life's trials and tribulations." She could be angry, yes, but without the very to describe the intensity. A story handed down to her apos was that when the family was rushing to leave home due to the rumored Japanese penetration (war time era), mother told everybody to wait because, said she, "I still have to brush my teeth." To this day, I remain wondering what strong wind could possibly rock her boat.

Mother was so punctilious — scrupulously clean in word, in thought, and in deed. I never heard her curse nor utter an unprintable. Gee, I'm raising her to high heavens with this remembrance, but I believe that's where she is now in the afterlife. Every night, she would gather the family for the rosary, and my brothers, who were notorious for dosing off during prayer time, would get a gentle reprimand.

From the perspective of one who is a mother herself, and now a grandmother of four, all my siblings and I have shown our house helpers mother's own kindness and consideration. Like mother, like children — I believe this would be the best way to honor our mother: to preserve and observe her values.

A stand-out in her character was her disbelief of superstitions. Like her own mother, i.e., our grandma, she threw superstitious beliefs into the garbage bin, so did we her children. She held on to the view that superstitions hinder the march of science, agree or disagree.

Would I say mine was the best Mom in the world? Mother had her own share of shortcomings, but I wouldn't want to delve into that now.

Some have dismissed Mother's Day because of its commercial value. More occasions, more anniversaries, more celebrations redound to more greeting cards, more gifts, more blowouts, more festivities. Good for the consumerist society — a whopping profit for business, albeit bad for those who go beyond the bounds of the purse. But of course, everyday can be a Mother's Day when Mom's values are held sacred as her offspring's guideposts in life.

In whatever tongue it it spoken, I daresay, Mother is a magical, awesome, sweet word to utter. juliaclagoc@yahoo.com

=====

Julia Carreon-Lagoc was a columnist of PANAY NEWS for two decades. She pops up with Accents now and then.

ooooo

18
Are We Prepared for Manmade Chaos

Erick San Juan
Sept 9, 2017

A real war is like a thief in the night. Nobody will be told or ask to prepare.

Although a country's leader should take the cue from the continuous word war from the current spat between US President Donald Trump (and the people in his loop) and North Korean leader Kim Jong-un.

But one can't help but ask - there are so many missing links that must be answered. Why is Kim and Trump telegraphing their punches? Who will strike first?

"The North Korean nuclear test last September 4, its sixth and most powerful, has once again exposed the extremely volatile and precarious state of global geopolitics and the great danger of a descent into a nuclear world war.

The unstable regime in Pyongyang has concluded that its only hope of self-preservation, in the face of provocative threats from a perceived unstable Trump administration, is to try and expand its nuclear arsenal as quickly as possible. North Korean leader Kim Jong-un is acutely conscious of the brutal end of Iraq's Saddam Hussein and Libya's Muammar Gaddafi, after they abandoned their so-called weapons of mass destruction.

While the actions of North Korea are certainly compounding the risk of conflict, prime responsibility for pushing the world to the brink of nuclear war rests with US imperialism. Moreover, as the (deliberate) reckless and belligerent statements from Trump and his officials demonstrate, North Korea's limited nuclear weaponry and reactionary nationalist bombast will not prevent the US from using its military might, including its huge nuclear arsenal, against the North Korean people.

Question is, whose funding and supplying Kim Jong-un' s technology and firepower?

After a meeting between Trump and his top military and national security advisers, US Defense Secretary James "Mad Dog" Mattis warned North Korea that it face "a massive military response" to any threat to the US or its allies.

"We are not looking to the total annihilation of a country, namely North Korea," Mattis continued, "but as I said, we have many options to do so." President Trump "wanted to be briefed on each one of them," he added.

I believe the statement of Secretary Mattis that they have a more superior technology controlled by the consortium of the military industrial complex. The so called killing mchine without destroying a nation's ecology. They even have killer robots and drones just like in the movies.

Trump himself warned of a US nuclear attack against North Korea when he declared last month that it confronted "fire and fury like the world has never seen." A White House readout from his phone call yesterday with Japanese Prime Minister Shinzo Abe explicitly declared that the US stood ready to use "the full range of diplomatic, conventional and nuclear capabilities at our disposal."

Trump was asked on Sunday:

"Will you attack North Korea?"

He refused to rule out pre-emptive military strikes, simply declaring: "We'll see."

The US president has repeatedly said that he would not signal a military attack in advance, compounding the uncertainty, and hence fears in Pyongyang.

Furthermore, as the crisis on the Korean Peninsula has escalated, the divisions in the Trump administration have resulted in an incoherent policy, which swings wildly between threats of all-out war and suggestions of talks, further inflaming the already explosive situation. This 'moro-moro' or political circus in the US political spectrum could be stage managed to make believe that the US government is in disarray and pretending to be weak. And this could provoke it's enemies to act while the US is in internal turmoil including the so called believed to be 'weather engineered&# 39; hurricanes destroying states like Texas.

In the aftermath of yesterday's nuclear test, the White House, along with the American media, has turned its fire on China and Russia, underscoring the fact that the US confrontation with North Korea is bound up with far broader strategic aims. American strategists regard domination of the vast Eurasian land mass as the key to US global hegemony and China as the chief obstacle to that goal. (Trump, North Korea and the Danger of World War, By Peter Symonds, Global Research, September 05, 2017)

That is in the area of geopolitics but we overlooked the fact that their (big nations) countries' economy are already overheating despite the propaganda that everything is well and healthy especially in the case of China. The full page advertisements in our major dailies (Manila Bulletin and Philippine Star) and other nations major dailies show how healthy is China's economic condition. But is it the truth or another 'fake news'? Just asking.

Another point raised by Peter Symonds (in the same article) – "The most dangerous factor in this highly volatile situation is the profound economic, social and political crisis of US imperialism—of which Trump is the most malignant expression. His administration confronts deep internal divisions and a huge and mounting social crisis, which is generating massive domestic opposition, as a result of its incompetence and indifference to the human suffering caused by the Houston flooding. The danger is that Trump will resort to a war against North Korea with incalculable consequences, as a means of directing acute domestic class tensions outwards against an external foe.

At the same time, these social tensions, in America and around the world, are fueling the coming revolutionary upheavals of the working class. The crucial issue is the building of a revolutionary leadership, to forge a unified international movement of workers guided by a scientific socialist program and perspective to put an end to the capitalist system and its outmoded division of the world into rival nation states. That is the perspective for which the International Committee of the Fourth International and its sections fight."

And there is another perspective pointed out by Stephen Lendman on the same issue – "Regardless of current or likely more advanced

DPRK capability later on, the nation's history shows it threatens no other nations.

Its nuclear and ballistic missile weapons are solely for defense – deterrents against feared US aggression.

The real menace lies in Washington, not Pyongyang. (Posted @Global Research, August 16, 2017)

For whatever it's worth the world is in the brink of another world war and sadly our domestic word war among politicians is also on the brink of an internal revolution. Are we ready for a new 'Bolshevik Revolution&# 39; through a revolutionary government? Are we prepared for a domestic revolution and the war against the real target of the globalist?

Just asking..

ooooo

19
Why I Publish/Reprint Books
Tatay Jobo Elizes
Self-Publisher

Writings are timeless and they act as mirrors to history. I publish writings as they remain relevant anytime. I have seen a lot of good writings in the internet, in magazines and newspapers. But most writers have only one or two articles and therefore not enough material to be published as a book. And yet, many of them need to be published or archived. There are also writers who write a lot but never publish them. There are also old books with no more prints available. The solution is to publish/reprint.

I do this for free because of the print-books-on-demand (POD) system, but the printed or hardcopy is not free

The printed book will always be there among your collections or libraries. Not all use the internet. The internet access has its technical problems. I can produce fiction, non-fiction, in color also.

My booklist can be seen at http://tinyurl.com/mj76ccq (copy and paste)

Permission had been granted by the author/authors to print their books under my free self-publishing service. They own copyrights to their works.

Interested reader may request free reading of any of my books, articles or essays via online reading or ebook. Just email me.

Thank you.

ooooo

www.ingramcontent.com/pod-product-compliance
Lightning Source LLC
Chambersburg PA
CBHW070814240726
48654CB00007B/342